dumb
employed

hilariously dumb
and sadly true
stories about
jobs like yours

phil edwards and matt kraft

RUNNING PRESS
PHILADELPHIA • LONDON

Books published by Running Press are available at special discounts for bulk purchases in the United States by corporations, institutions, and other organizations.
For more information, please contact the Special Markets Department at the
Perseus Books Group, 2300 Chestnut Street, Suite 200, Philadelphia, PA 19103,
or call (800) 810-4145, ext. 5000, or email special.markets@perseusbooks.com.

ISBN 978-0-7624-4238-6
Library of Congress Control Number: 2010937353

E-book ISBN 978-0-7624-4323-9

9   8   7   6   5   4   3   2   1
Digit on the right indicates the number of this printing

Cover design, tips, and charts by Phil Edwards and Matt Kraft
Interior design by Bill Jones
Typography: Helvetica, Deluxe Gothic, Giovanni, Mufferaw, Tekton,
and Spunky Jes

Running Press Book Publishers
2300 Chestnut Street
Philadelphia, PA 19103-4371

Visit us on the web!
www.runningpress.com
www.dumbemployed.com

CONTENTS

INTRODUCTION

There's a word for the work you do.

Believe it or not, you aren't the only one sipping the bitter cocktail of boredom and frustration that is your job. Work feels like work for just about everyone. Employment pollsters report that 92 percent of all people are unhappy at their jobs and the other 8 percent are lying. As for the pollsters, they're all looking for new work as soon as possible.

It's not just one thing that makes your job terrible—it's a mix as delectable as Dr. Pepper on your Chex Mix. There are a thousand things to blame—though you should never blame yourself, of course. That twitchy feeling you get as soon as you punch your time card or step inside your office lobby? It's not because you have deep-seated issues with responsibility and the necessary concessions of adult life. It's because your job sucks.

Like cartographers in hell, we've mapped out the five factors that make your job so infuriatingly dumb: Bosses, Customers, Just Dumb, Overtime, and Weird Shift. In each section, we chart your misery with blistering accuracy and a whole mess of testimonials because, as we mentioned before, you are not alone.

We'll give you glimpses of work at its worst, tips on how to make it through another day, and a whole host of pretty pictures that will make you feel slightly better about your own job (or at least distract you from that boring Excel spreadsheet). All these elements define modern work. Whether you're in a fast food kitchen or a corporate office, a truck stop or a law firm, or an office park or a trailer park, you know what it means to be frustrated. It doesn't matter if your job requires brains or brawn, or if you're a CEO or an intern. We all have the same complaints in common, and they're not going to change anytime soon.

We know that you're part of it, too. That's why you'll have space to write your very own on-the-job sagas at the end of each chapter. We're sure that you have stories to share, record, and remember—although we aren't sure that there's enough space in any book to fit all of them between two covers.

Fortunately, there's a word for what you go through. There's a word for what you, your friends, your family members, and even your enemies face every time you drag yourself out of bed, clock in and out day after day, show up at nine a.m. on the dot, and fill out your taxes. There's a word for what you are, and this book is our way to offer our condolences.

It's time for you to face the truth and confirm what thousands of people have already realized before you. Just sit back, relax, and take a deep breath, because there's only one word that defines what you do.

You're dumbemployed.

BOSSES

Bosses are as inevitable as death and taxes, but they aren't quite as forgiving. You can look forward to a lifetime spent laughing at your boss's mediocre jokes, dodging his bad breath, and trying not to come up with better ideas than his. Assuming you survive the gauntlet, your reward will be a promotion with a newer, worse boss you hate even more, in addition to underlings that can't stand you.

AT WORK TODAY, MY BOSS GAVE ME SOME INSTRUCTIONS ON MY RECENT REPORT ON GLOBAL CORN FUTURES. HIS FIRST WAS TO MAKE IT SHORTER. HIS SECOND WAS TO MAKE IT LOCAL. AND HIS THIRD WAS TO MAKE IT ABOUT SOY INSTEAD OF CORN. I'M DUMBEMPLOYED.

At work today, I was interviewing for a higher position at my company. My boss introduced me glowingly—so glowingly, in fact, that she said she "didn't believe any of the bad things people were saying." I'm dumbemployed.

At work today, my "team" and I met around one of the small tables in our restaurant. Our shift manager came in and slowly poured water on the table. "This team," he said, "is the glass. Without it, we spill." Great metaphor, boss. Then he made us clean it up. I'm dumbemployed.

At work today, my boss asked us if we had any questions about the new system for stocking shelves. I asked him something about alphabetical order. "I meant good questions," he said. But I think he just didn't know the answer. I'm dumbemployed.

At work today, I scheduled a vacation trip for my boss. It's not my job, but whatever. The bad part was that he asked me afterward to make it "more fun." The trip was to rural Wisconsin. Should I have included cow tipping? I'm dumbemployed.

At work today, the guy I work for told me that I "really need to show some maturity." He's my fast food manager and was exactly one grade above me in high school—after he was held back a year. I'm dumbemployed.

Tip

Your boss may be stupid, but remember that's also the reason you were hired.

AT WORK TODAY, MY CHEAPSKATE BOSS MADE ME BOTH COOK A MEAL AND BAKE A TRAY OF BROWNIES. I'M NOT GOOD UNDER PRESSURE—HALFWAY THROUGH, I REALIZED I WAS BAKING BUTTER AND SAUTÉING WITH BROWNIE MIX. CAN I HAVE MY NAP NOW? I'M DUMBEMPLOYED.

At work today, my boss was sweeping outside, which is my job. I asked him why and he said he wanted to "keep in touch with the little people." I'm dumbemployed.

At work today, my supervisor called us into the break room for a meeting. "All hands on deck," he said. "We need to talk about cleaning bathrooms." I didn't realize that when he said "deck," he meant the poop deck. I'm dumbemployed.

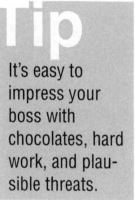

It's easy to impress your boss with chocolates, hard work, and plausible threats.

At work today, I was making a profit-and-loss spreadsheet. "Great, we're in the red!" my boss shouted when he saw it. Then I pointed out that red is bad. "Oh," he said and frowned. "I always get those mixed up." I'm dumbemployed.

At work today, my boss actually had me pick him up Pepto-Bismol at the store. My title is vice president of marketing, but it should be vice president of babysitting. I'm dumbemployed.

AT WORK TODAY, MY SUPERVISOR OFFERED ME A CORONA IN THE BREAK ROOM. I APPRECIATED THE GESTURE—BUT I'M NOT SURE IF THAT'S REALLY APPROPRIATE FOR OUR DAYCARE CENTER. I'M DUMBEMPLOYED.

BEHAVIOR WITH BOSS WATCHING OVER SHOULDER

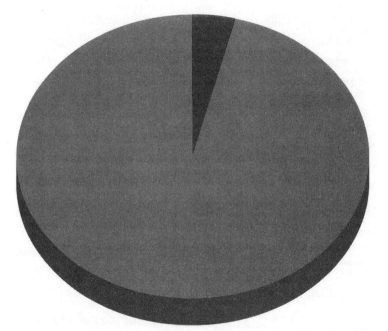

- ■ WORKING
- ■ PRETENDING TO WORK

At work today, the dentist I work for said we should push glow-in-the-dark floss on our patients, because he wants to "mack on" the sales representative. Some quality care, doctor. I'm dumbemployed.

At work today, I filled out three index cards with my talking points for an afternoon presentation. I returned to find my boss looking through them. He then used them for his own presentation and I was left to mutter. I'm dumbemployed.

At work today, we had an office party to celebrate my coworker's new sales. Of course, my boss bought the "champagne." How many times do I have to tell him that sparkling apple cider is not champagne? I'm dumbemployed.

At work today, I realized I've been working at my current office for five and a half years. In that period of time, the president and I have had two conversations—both of which were in the elevator when he asked me to move out of his way. I'm dumbemployed.

AT WORK TODAY, MY SUPERVISOR HAD ME PRICING ORANGES IN THE PRODUCE AISLE. HE TOLD ME I DID IT WRONG—THEN HE REALIZED THAT HE HAD CONFUSED ORANGES AND TANGERINES. I HAD TO DO IT OVER. I'M DUMBEMPLOYED.

At work today, I started as a lawyer. Three years of law school, two major internships, and one job finally begun. My first duty? Interpreting a senior partner's coffee order. I'm dumb-employed.

Tip

There's a reason you've never seen your boss and the devil in a room at the same time.

At work today, my boss had a housewarming party. He and his wife live in a palace in the sky with leather chairs and a huge plasma TV. Naturally, he spent half the party talking about how "cutbacks will be an inevitability." I'm dumbemployed.

At work today, I was writing copy for a brochure about our services. My boss came by and said, "I think you flipped the clauses here." He was pointing at a one-clause sentence. I'm dumbemployed.

CAN YOUR BOSS READ?

At work today, my manager had me write thank-you notes to 312 regional suppliers. I know his signature so well that I could probably forge a check. Hmm, I think I'll go do that right now. I'm dumbemployed.

AT WORK TODAY, MY BOSS CHIDED ME FOR MAKING "SMALL TALK" IN THE HALLWAY AT WORK. ALL I DID TODAY WAS SPEND FIVE MINUTES ASKING MY COWORKER ABOUT A WORK PROJECT. APPARENTLY, EVEN ON-TASK DISCUSSION IS ILLEGAL NOW. I'M DUMBEMPLOYED.

At work today, I showed up five minutes late due to road construction. "I told you to get an SUV," my boss said. "You need to take the drive into your own hands." Sorry, sir—I'm not risking my life to make fast food. I'm dumbemployed.

At work today, my boss, whose jean shorts aren't exactly the height of sophistication, spent about twenty minutes making fun of "the hicks in Nebraska." That would be funny—but we live in Kansas. I'm dumbemployed.

At work today, my boss made the grand announcement that he had bought us a rice cooker for the kitchen. That would be really cool—except that we were kind of hoping he'd buy a microwave first. I'm dumbemployed.

At work today, there were about one hundred phone calls coming into our telemarketing center because our product was featured on the local news a couple of times. My boss was ecstatic. Then I reminded him that the news stories were about a recall. I'm dumbemployed.

At work today, I was working the returns desk. My boss leaned over my shoulder the entire time and then criticized me for "grilling" the customer. All I did was ask for a receipt—which I'd be fired for not having. I'm dumbemployed.

At work today, I was talking with a coworker about the Jets. My boss sidled up to us and started laughing. "I'm a fan of Bennie." It took us five minutes to get the joke. But we laughed right away—we had to. I'm dumbemployed.

At work today, my boss showed up with an intense haircut. Now I feel morally obligated to give him an update on the status of the mullet. Sir, it's still dead. I'm dumbemployed.

At work today, we were doing icebreakers around the office and asked what everybody's favorite Beatles song was. My boss's answer? "Satisfaction." No one corrected him. I'm dumbemployed.

Tip

If you have a boss who likes golf, shouting "Fore!" around the office is a great way to get his attention.

At work today, my boss came in dressed like a cowboy with boots, a leather vest, and a hat. The reason? He's going apple-picking after work. This is the man I work for. I'm dumbemployed.

At work today, my boss decided that it's part of my duties to clean out his pickup truck. That would be fine, if it weren't for the fact that he's a hunter. Now I smell like a deer. I'm dumbemployed.

At work today, I double-bagged a customer's groceries, at her request. I was later called aside by my boss for "wasting resources." Last time I checked, a paper bag cost about a tenth of a cent. I'm dumbemployed.

At work today, my boss said that our competitors deserved "a new square of hell." I'm pretty sure the expression is "a new circle of hell." But maybe that's why they're killing us in the marketplace. I'm dumbemployed.

Tip

You may want to kill your boss, but simply kidnapping him may be sufficient.

At work today, I was folding blue jeans. My supervisor tapped me on the shoulder gently and asked me where I'd learned how to fold. She spent twenty minutes showing me the "right way" without realizing she was the one who'd taught me the "wrong way" eight months before. I'm dumbemployed.

At work today, I catered a Bar Mitzvah and had snobby thirteen-year-olds ask for more cheese. My manager saw me and told me to "sex it up a little." I'm dumbemployed.

AT WORK TODAY, I WAS WORKING OUT OF A COFFEE SHOP IN ORDER TO FOCUS ON A VERY TOUGH PROJECT. MY BOSS'S REPLY TO MY MEDITATIVE MISSION? "GET ME A DECAF MOCHA LATTE WITH CINNAMON SPRINKLES." I'M DUMBEMPLOYED.

At work today, I got a chance to decorate my own office. It was a momentous occasion, until my boss palmed a framed picture of my daughter and asked me who the hot chick was. I'm dumbemployed.

Tip

Friends with your boss on Facebook? Make sure to tag yourself in pictures where you're drinking and doing drugs so that he knows how cool you are.

At work today, I was selling concessions and gave a customer three ketchup packets, which resulted in my supervisor yelling at me. Apparently, two is the maximum, and my pay will be docked for the third. I'm dumbemployed.

At work today, the company taxes were being organized and filed. Fun stuff. That's also when I discovered that my boss flew first class as he was downsizing the company. I'm dumbemployed.

Tip

It's always good to protect yourself in the workplace. Play it safe and force your boss to show you identification each time you meet.

At work today, a very overweight man and woman came into our restaurant and sat down. They were incredibly rude to me and insisted on two bottles of ketchup, one for each of them. Only later did I learn that they were my manager's relatives. I'm dumbemployed.

AT WORK TODAY, MY SUPERVISOR INSISTED THAT WE INSTITUTE A NUMBER SYSTEM IN ORDER TO DEAL WITH OUR OVERFLOW OF CUSTOMERS. WE DID IT—AND REACHED NO. 4 BY THE END OF THE DAY. I'M DUMBEMPLOYED.

At work today, I was standing in front of a bland piece of corporate art in our lobby. My boss sidled up beside me and nodded his head. "It's about sex," he said. I had to agree. I'm dumbemployed.

At work today, I was drinking a weird soda that I bought at a special grocery store. My boss saw me and asked for a sip, which he took directly from my can. Then he sneezed on it. I'm dumbemployed.

At work today, my boss asked me if we should create a mobile app for our store. We sell yarn. I don't think our customers know what apps are. I'm dumbemployed.

At work today, I was setting up for a gig, where I guess the bar's owner is my boss. He asked me if my band could play an Elton John cover during the gig. We are a metal band. I'm dumbemployed.

At work today, my boss asked me if I enjoyed baseball. I told him I do, so he asked me to explain it to him before a meeting with a client who is a big fan. Ten minutes in, he quit because it was too boring. I'm dumbemployed.

At work today, I brought my new cell phone into work. It was $200 with a two-year contract. My boss decided it would be funny to dangle it over the coffee pot. That's when he dropped it in by accident. I'm dumbemployed.

AT WORK TODAY, MY BOSS WALKED AROUND THE OFFICE LIMPING AND HINTING ALL DAY, "IF ONLY SOMEBODY COULD CRACK MY ACHING BACK, I'D FEEL SO MUCH BETTER." FIVE MINUTES LATER, I WAS LIFTING MY SUPERIOR INTO THE AIR. I'M DUMBEMPLOYED.

At work today, my office moved from building A to building B. My boss did a great job supervising the moving process. He sat in a lawn chair between the two and drank from a suspicious-looking glass. I'm dumbemployed.

AT WORK TODAY, I LEFT MY BRIEFCASE ON THE BUS. I WAS TELLING MY COWORKERS ABOUT IT WHEN MY BOSS CAME BY AND REPRIMANDED ME FOR A POTENTIAL "SECURITY BREACH." A SECURITY BREACH? I SELL MULCH TO LANDSCAPERS. I'M DUMBEMPLOYED.

At work today, I was eating an avocado during my break when my manager peered over my shoulder. He told me that my "pear" looked rotten. I'm dumbemployed.

At work today, I heard ABBA in the office, blasting loudly for at least an hour and a half. Guess whose boss just got speakers for his computer? I'm dumbemployed.

At work today, I was on my usual walk to work when I spotted my boss across the street and heading in my direction. I went about fifteen minutes out of my way just to ensure I wouldn't have to walk with him into our building. I'm dumbemployed.

DRESS FOR SUCCESS

- It may be tempting to wear a short skirt and low-cut dress just to get ahead. However, remember that most men simply don't look good in those types of clothes.

- A well tied tie can double as a noose.

- For important meetings, you should always wear a jacket. If you don't have a suit jacket, a down coat will do the trick.

- People judge you by what you wear, like it or not. That's a good reason to expense all of your clothing purchases to the company credit card.

- Fedoras went out of style in the '50s. But trucker hats? Never.

- A shoe shine is a great way to get a brief high from shoe polish fumes. Do it at least twice a day.

- Always wear an undershirt so that when you rip your top shirt off in anger, you won't be half nude.

At work today, the elevator was especially packed. While breathing in Old Spice and hash browns, I felt a hand on the back of my skirt. When we got out of the elevator, I realized that it had been my boss. I'm dumbemployed.

At work today, I was checking out a girl who walked into our store. My supervisor told me she was his cousin, so I didn't hit on her. Then my supervisor did. He'd lied just to throw me off my game. It's the most leadership he's ever shown. I'm dumbemployed.

tip

If you want to be your own boss, the first step is learning to hate yourself.

At work today, I was setting up our bookstore for a reading. I love the author, Salman Rushdie, and told my manager about it. He then pronounced his name like it was the fish. I'm dumbemployed.

AT WORK TODAY, I HAD TO SPRINT TO CATCH A LOVELY OLD WOMAN WHO LEFT HER CREDIT CARD AT MY REGISTER. MY BOSS THEN SCOLDED ME FOR RUNNING AFTER HER THROUGH THE STORE. MAYBE HE WANTED TO STEAL HER CREDIT CARD. I'M DUMBEMPLOYED.

At work today, my boss told me that I shouldn't come into the bar dressed like a nun. I was wearing a skirt that went an inch below my knee. I'm dumbemployed.

AT WORK TODAY, MY MANAGER REQUESTED I MODIFY MY EGG-FRYING TECHNIQUE TO FIT MORE EGGS INTO THE PAN. I CURRENTLY DO FOUR AT A TIME. AM I SUPPOSED TO LAYER THEM? I'M DUMBEMPLOYED.

At work today, I heard a ringing noise and assumed that it was my alarm clock. It wasn't. It was my boss calling to make sure I got to work on time. I wasn't aware he had that duty now. I'm dumbemployed.

At work today, my boss said we had to ask customers whether they wanted our "Everglade Snow" coffee blend or our "Rustic Bean" variety. I watched him pour the same batch of coffee into both containers. I'm dumbemployed.

At work today, I was canvassing theater listings for something to see. My boss saw me and invited me to see him perform poetry. This is from the man who can't even compose an email without a smiley face. I'm in for a long night. I'm dumbemployed.

At work today, my supervisor took me on a helicopter so that we could look at potential construction sites. It would have been cool, but it was so loud that he had to keep his mouth against my ear so that I could hear him. Intimate, huh? I'm dumbemployed.

At work today, we were dealing with a recall of over a million cars. Naturally, customers weren't particularly happy when they called. My boss, however, said it was a selling opportunity. To me, that's not what deadly vehicles lead to. I'm dumbemployed.

Tip

A boss can be a great father figure, especially if you sit on his lap.

At work today, the owner of our company tried to guide me with a long parable about fishermen and fishes. Shouldn't he know that a twenty-four-year-old woman might not be the best audience for that? I'm dumbemployed.

At work today, my boss decided he'd wear jeans to work. I just wish he'd worn a belt, too. I'm dumbemployed.

At work today, my boss was nice enough to take us out for drinks. Cool, right? Less cool was that he ordered everyone Diet Cokes to save money. I'm dumbemployed.

AT WORK TODAY, MY BOSS SENT ME TO A TENANT'S APARTMENT TO FIX THE WATER PRESSURE. BEFORE-HAND, HE TOLD ME NOT TO DO TOO GOOD A JOB, SINCE THE TENANT WAS MOVING OUT IN TWO MONTHS. I'M DUMBEMPLOYED.

At work today, our assistant manager said that we were in a "Defcon situation" and she needed to take over for the day. Call me crazy, but I don't think Defcon involves table settings. I'm dumbemployed.

At work today, my supervisor sent me and my limo to take an eight-year-old kid to the airport. My boss warned me to be especially nice so I'd get a good tip. What would an eight-year-old tip me? Gummy bears? I'm dumbemployed.

AT WORK TODAY, I KINDLY GAVE MY BOSS A CUP OF COFFEE, WHICH IS, FOR THE RECORD, NOT MY JOB. HE RESPONDED BY ASKING ME TO HURRY BACK WITH SUGAR, CREAM, AND A DASH OF HONEY. I'M DUMBEMPLOYED.

At work today, I had to meet with sales guys to talk about my engineering work. They immediately asked me to make something that sells better. I thought that was their job. I'm dumbemployed.

At work today, we installed an Xbox in our office break room. The first email about it said that we shouldn't spend more than five minutes playing it. What game is that short? Now the box just taunts me. I'm dumbemployed.

At work today, my boss's four-year-old son came in to work and sat near my desk. "Daddy told me about you," he said. "You're the one who is filling space." I'm dumbemployed.

AT WORK TODAY, THERE WAS A VERY SMALL EARTHQUAKE IN OUR BUILDING, WHICH IS TYPICAL IN LA. A FEW HOURS LATER, I FOUND MY BOSS STILL COWERING IN A DOORFRAME, SHAKING. I'M DUMBEMPLOYED.

At work today, my watch stopped, so I had to rely on my cell phone for the time. My supervisor saw me take it out and asked me whom I was sexting with. I'm dumbemployed.

At work today, the assistant manager decided that he would make a power play and tell me what to do. I can understand jockeying for dominance at work. But did he have to make me literally bow down before him? I'm dumbemployed.

AT WORK TODAY, I INTERVIEWED A PROSPECTIVE RECEPTIONIST. AFTERWARDS, MY BOSS ASKED ME TO RATE HER ON A SCALE OF ONE TO TEN. I RELUCTANTLY DID—AFTER WHICH MY BOSS CALLED ME A SEXIST FOR NOT RATING HER HIGHER. I'M DUMBEMPLOYED.

Tip

If you have a female manager, she'd probably prefer that you call her a womanager instead.

At work today, there was thick fog as I drove in. As a result, I cut a black jeep off. When I reached work, I saw my boss step out of the jeep. Now so he doesn't hate me, I'll have to hide my car as long as I work here. I'm dumbemployed.

At work today, I was asked to get concert tickets for my boss's teenage daughter. Never mind that I shouldn't be doing that in the first place. My boss also gave me fifty bucks less than I needed. I'm dumbemployed.

At work today, my boss was doing a crossword puzzle and needed a four-letter word for "stupid." I told him "dumb." But "boss" would have worked, too. I'm dumbemployed.

At work today, the door to my office was locked, so a VP offered to jimmy it open. An hour later, I had a broken door lock and a sweaty VP. I'm dumbemployed.

At work today, my boss asked me to lend him a pen. This is the third he's stolen from me, yet he's the one who complains that our office supplies budget is inflated. I'm dumbemployed.

At work today, my boss's son took over as my new supervisor. He has two fewer degrees than I do and didn't know how to log into his computer. I'm dumbemployed.

AT WORK TODAY, MY BOSS INVITED US TO COME WITH HIM ON HIS BOAT. I EXPECTED A YACHT. I SPENT TWO HOURS ON A GLORIFIED CANOE. I'M DUMBEMPLOYED.

AT WORK TODAY, WE INSTALLED AN AIR CONDITIONER IN OUR OFFICE. THE OWNER IS SO CHEAP, HOWEVER, THAT HE SET IT TO EIGHTY DEGREES. I'M DUMBEMPLOYED.

At work today, I listened to a lecture about the importance of presentation. It was given by my boss, who was wearing a neon pink tie with a bright green shirt. I'm dumbemployed.

Tip

It's a good idea to try and squeeze a holiday bonus from your boss. Pretend you're an eleven-year-old urchin so she feels sorry for you.

At work today, my immediate superior asked me to start calling him by his full title. As far as I know, it's "cashier." Somehow, I'm lower than that. I'm dumbemployed.

At work today, there was a cold going around the office. Naturally, my boss said it was passed through kissing. There are only three people in the office. So it was kind of creepy. I'm dumbemployed.

HOW YOUR BOSS SPENDS HIS TIME

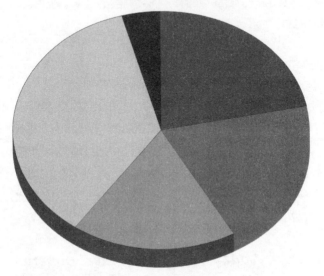

■ PLOTS AGAINST YOU

■ POWER NAPS

■ PLAYS MINESWEEPER

■ THINKS UP JOKES FOR
THE WATER COOLER

■ WORKS

At work today, the owner of our company brought her three cats in to work. I'm deathly allergic, but I was forced to pet—and nuzzle—each one. I'm dumbemployed.

At work today, I saw my ex-girl-friend around the office. It turns out she's dating my boss. They met at a company picnic that I brought her to when we were still going out. I'm dumbemployed.

AT WORK TODAY, MY MANAGER OFFERED ME A KLEENEX WHEN I SNEEZED. ONLY AFTERWARDS DID I REALIZE THAT IT HAD BEEN USED. I'M DUMBEMPLOYED.

Tip

If you want to get on your boss's good side, start calling him "Master" in a creepy voice.

At work today, my boss asked me whom I was voting for in a local election. I told him that was private. He said I was un-American for saying that. I'm dumbemployed.

At work today, a new era began. My boss didn't wear a sweater vest for the first time since I've known him. But we've got a long way to go. Now we need him to wear something other than a bow tie. I'm dumbemployed.

At work today, my boss said that he'd forward me some good news. It was a rejection from a client. I asked what the heck the good news was. He told me the rejection had great feedback. I'm dumbemployed.

Tip

If your boss receives a "World's Best Boss" mug, remember that the United Nations has to authenticate the claim.

AT WORK TODAY, MY NEW BOSS EMAILED THE ENTIRE OFFICE WITH A GUIDELINE ABOUT HOW TO PRONOUNCE HIS NAME. IT WAS FOUR PARAGRAPHS LONG AND I STILL DON'T KNOW HOW TO SAY HIS NAME. I'M DUMBEMPLOYED.

At work today, my coworker wore his team jersey into the office to celebrate the playoffs. My boss physically hit him when he saw it and didn't even think to apologize. I'm dumbemployed.

At work today, a second Amendment rights group chose to protest in our custard store. Instead of kicking them out, my boss joined them with his own gun. I'm dumbemployed.

At work today, my boss asked to borrow my car jack to change his tire. Then he asked me to change his tire for him. I'm dumbemployed.

At work today, my manager claimed he is one of the best "keytar" players in the county. I assume there's not a lot of competition. I'm dumbemployed.

At work today, my boss said that he was instituting a long-term plan for the next two weeks. If two weeks is long-term, you might have a problem. I'm dumbemployed.

AT WORK TODAY, THERE WAS A CAVEAT TO THE RAISE MY BOSS OFFERED ME. IT'S NOT SUPPOSED TO KICK IN FOR ANOTHER TWO YEARS. I'M DUMB-EMPLOYED.

Tip

If you want to rise through the ranks, try convincing your boss that you're his son.

At work today, my manager called us all to the front of the store to see our new sign. That was when we notified him that "Miscelaneous" should have two l's in it. I'm dumbemployed.

At work today, I told my boss I was getting a new queen-size bed for my wife and me. He said I should spring for a king. I then asked him what he had, and he admitted he still sleeps in a twin. I'm dumbemployed.

At work today, my boss asked me and my coworker to lunch, which he referred to as a "threesome." I'm dumbemployed.

AT WORK TODAY, MY BOSS ASKED ME IF IT WAS "THAT TIME OF THE MONTH." THAT WOULD BE INAPPROPRIATE AT ANY TIME, BUT SINCE I'M SEVEN MONTHS PREGNANT, IT DOESN'T EVEN MAKE SENSE. I'M DUMBEMPLOYED.

Tip

It's best not to call your boss after ten, so show up at her house instead.

At work today, my supervisor brought a newspaper to work and asked us if we'd seen the paper today. We work in a Web development firm—of course we haven't seen it. I'm dumbemployed.

At work today, our director of marketing was bragging that he is a man of letters and loves intellectual pursuits. Except, instead of "intellectual," he said "inctellectish." I'm dumbemployed.

JOB INTERVIEW DEALBREAKERS

The second recommendation is from my parole officer. He's so lenient!

You know, in many cultures, interviews begin with an exchange of gifts—or fluids.

What's my greatest weakness? Kryptonite.

One other question: what specific drugs will the drug test cover?

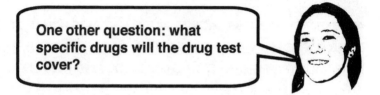

At work today, we attached a spigot to a hose outside. My boss was overjoyed and said now we don't have to install a sink in the shop. I'm dumbemployed.

At work today, our manager gave us the default customer service reply. Basically, we're supposed to deny the problem, even if we don't know what it is. I'm dumbemployed.

AT WORK TODAY, I DISCOVERED HOW MUCH OF A MINIMALIST MY BOSS IS. OUR OFFICE GOT REDECORATED AND NOW MY DESK IS A STACK OF LIQUOR CRATES. I'M DUMBEMPLOYED.

At work today, smoke came out of our kitchen and my boss emerged eyebrowless. He said that it was all part of his plan. I'm dumbemployed.

At work today, my boss asked me how many chips I thought our computers should have. Sir, that's not how it works. I'm dumbemployed.

AT WORK TODAY, MY MANAGER INVITED US TO HIS HOUSE FOR DRINKS. EXCEPT WHEN HE MEANT TO SAY "COCKTAILS," HE INVITED US OVER FOR "CROUTONS." I'M DUMBEMPLOYED.

At work today, the HR director presented me with a choice between a job in New York or Chicago. I live in Pittsburgh and told her it would be a struggle. She said she could decide for me, if I wanted. I'm dumbemployed.

At work today, I was told my boss's daughter was coming in to tour the office. I saw a young woman and asked if her dad was around. Later, I found out she was my boss's girlfriend. I'm dumbemployed.

Tip

Bosses love knowledgeable employees. Google yours and show him every single secret you've found.

At work today, my friend Jon and I were talking about movies when my boss sidled up. We kept talking and mentioned *The Godfather*. My boss tilted his head. "What's that one?" he asked. I'm dumbemployed.

At work today, our head of marketing said he wanted to buy ads in the newspaper to reach the young people. I told him young people don't read newspapers. "Well, we'll advertise in the young section," he responded. I'm dumbemployed.

At work today, I asked my manager what his favorite book was. My small talk started a five-minute rant about the "truth behind *The Da Vinci Code*." I'm dumbemployed.

At work today, our coordinator asked us to line up in a row and count off. I am thirty-two-years-old and I'm in preschool. I'm dumbemployed.

At work today, I served yet another day as chief coat checker. As a professional coat holder, I think I'm good. But my boss told me today that I have years to go until I "learn the art of it." I'm dumbemployed.

At work today, I stood behind my boss at the water fountain. Why is it that some people believe it's fine to fill an entire milk jug with one of the slowest faucets on earth? I'm dumbemployed.

AT WORK TODAY, MY BOSS TOLD ME I NEEDED TO CLEAN OUT THE RAT TRAP IN THE BACK OF THE BUILDING. I'VE NEVER DONE IT BEFORE. I CHECKED IT OUT AND GOT BITTEN BY A LIVE RAT. NOW I HAVE TO PAY FOR RABIES SHOTS WITH MY OWN MONEY. I'M DUMBEMPLOYED.

At work today, our manager asked that we begin making our office "greener." He said this with a Styrofoam coffee cup in his hand. I'm dumbemployed.

At work today, I emailed our owner to ask for a three-day weekend six months from now. He told me that I needed to give more notice. I'm dumbemployed.

At work today, I went into the bathroom and saw my barefoot boss with one foot on the sink. He was cutting his toenails. "Hygiene is crucial," he told me before continuing. I'm dumbemployed.

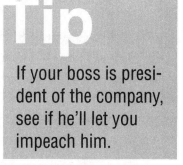

Tip

If your boss is president of the company, see if he'll let you impeach him.

At work today, my boss requested that we call him BJ instead of his full name. That would be fine, except that his name is Michael. I'm dumbemployed.

AT WORK TODAY, I SPILLED A LITTLE KETCHUP ON THE CORNER OF MY SUIT JACKET. MY BOSS THEN SQUIRTED SOME OF HIS KETCHUP ON THE OTHER SIDE SO THAT IT WOULD MATCH. THANKS. I'M DUMBEMPLOYED.

At work today, we had a meeting with the governor, though he was really just going from one place to another. Despite that, my boss shoved me into the man's face to start "networking." I'm dumbemployed.

At work today, my boss added me on Facebook, which I've come to expect. I didn't expect that he'd immediately start posting about politics and sex. I'm dumbemployed.

At work today, my boss asked if anybody in the office knew French. He needed to translate a chocolate bar he was about to eat. I'm dumbemployed.

AT WORK TODAY, MY MANAGER PULLED ME ASIDE AND TOLD ME HE WANTED TO TALK ABOUT MY BEING DISTRACTED AT WORK. I PROTESTED AND HE REALIZED HE'D ACTUALLY BEEN THINKING OF ANOTHER PERSON. I'M DUMBEMPLOYED.

At work today, I asked my boss if he'd consider writing me a letter of recommendation for grad school. He asked me why I wanted to go. Then I finished cooking the fries. I'm dumbemployed.

At work today, we were all milling around a coworker's desk watching a YouTube video. Then we heard my boss coming down the hall. I understand why roaches scatter. I'm dumbemployed.

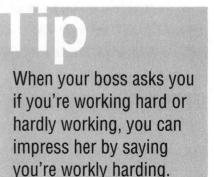

When your boss asks you if you're working hard or hardly working, you can impress her by saying you're workly harding.

At work today, our owner announced he's selling the company to the bank because of bankruptcy. This is the first time we heard anything was wrong. I'm dumbemployed.

AT WORK TODAY, I GAVE A DEPOSITION IN A SEXUAL HARASSMENT LAWSUIT AGAINST MY BOSS. I SPECIFICALLY REQUESTED THAT THE WORD "SKEEVY" BE ENTERED INTO THE RECORD. I'M DUMBEMPLOYED.

At work today, our chain restaurant decided to make us give toys with each meal. My boss took two for "testing purposes." We saw him playing with them later. I'm dumbemployed.

At work today, a superior asked me for help with an email that he was having trouble sending. "It just won't send!" he complained. I took a look at it; he was trying to send an email to, and I am not kidding, "www.gmail.com." I'm dumb-employed.

At work today, my boss moved me into a new office for the day. I thought it was a promotion, but he told me I had a special project. He booted up a computer and told me, "I want you to upgrade my character." He had turned on World of Warcraft and wanted me to play all day. I'm dumbemployed.

At work today, I suggested to my boss that we make the office a little "greener." He smiled and pointed at a calendar. "Don't you know that's what St. Patrick's Day is for?" I'm dumbemployed.

AT WORK TODAY, OUR MANAGER DECIDED TO CALL A MEETING AT EIGHT A.M., AND EVEN PEOPLE LIKE ME WITH A THREE P.M. SHIFT HAD TO SHOW UP. THE IMPORTANT MEETING'S SUBJECT? APPARENTLY, WE NEED TO USE PENCIL ON OUR TIME CARDS INSTEAD OF PEN. THE MEETING LASTED FIVE MINUTES. I'M DUMBEMPLOYED.

At work today, my supervisor asked me how to spell the word "first." I'm dumbemployed.

At work today, my boss locked herself in her office. I had to go through the hallway door (which was unlocked) and show her how to unlock her own door from the inside. I'm dumbemployed.

At work today, I told my commanding officer I'd need to go on Skype at three in order to talk to my wife. He asked me why. I told him my wife was pregnant. He said I should wait for something important to happen. I'm dumbemployed.

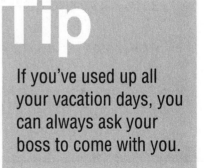

Tip

If you've used up all your vacation days, you can always ask your boss to come with you.

At work today, I was ordering my boss's lunch with a client. He said he wanted something light, so I ordered salads. He talked to me after the meeting, his face red. "When I say light," he huffed, "I mean that the steaks should be eight ounces instead of twelve." I'm dumbemployed.

At work today, I finally got my boss's recommendation for my grad school application. It took him three weeks to get it back to me. The text: "Joe works hard." That's all he wrote. I'm dumbemployed.

At work today, I came into work wearing a cardigan from a designer place. My boss saw me and tugged at my shoulders. "Hi, Mr. Rogers," he said and laughed. He stretched the fabric—which cost $112. I'm dumbemployed.

At work today, we got a kinda cool new webcam for the computer at the front desk. When I came back from lunch, I noticed that someone had made a video on it. I pressed "play." It turned out that my boss had practiced raising his right eyebrow for the camera. For twelve minutes. I'm dumbemployed.

At work today, I showed up to the office a little tipsy after lunch. Seeing as how it was my last day with the company, I figured a little celebration was in order. My boss took me aside, scolded me, and said, "This better not happen again, or you'll be let go." I'm dumbemployed.

At work today, the highlight of my day was taking the boss's car to the car wash. Is it sad that I find all the pretty brushes exciting? I'm dumbemployed.

At work today, I brought in some sea salt for the break room kitchen. My supervisor came in, picked up the can, and scowled. "Why don't you just boil ocean water?" he shouted. "What a waste of money." Okay boss, you do that. I'm dumb-employed.

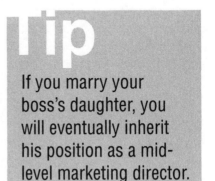

Tip

If you marry your boss's daughter, you will eventually inherit his position as a mid-level marketing director.

YOUR TURN!

At work today, _____

_____

_____

_____

_____

_____

_____

_____

_____I'm dumbemployed.

At work today, _____

_____

_____

_____

_____

_____

_____

_____I'm dumbemployed.

At work today, _____

_____

_____

_____

_____

_____

_____

_____I'm dumbemployed.

At work today, _____

_____

_____

_____

_____

_____

_____

_____I'm dumbemployed.

At work today, _____

_____

_____

_____

_____

_____

_____

_____

_____I'm dumbemployed.

At work today, _____

_____

_____

_____

_____

_____

_____

_____

_____I'm dumbemployed.

At work today, _____

_____

_____

_____

_____

_____

_____

_____

_____I'm dumbemployed.

At work today, _____

_____

_____

_____

_____

_____

_____

_____I'm dumbemployed.

At work today, _____

_____

_____

_____

_____

_____

_____

_____

_____I'm dumbemployed.

At work today, _____

_____

_____

_____

_____

_____

_____

_____

_____I'm dumbemployed.

CUSTOMERS

Customers don't just want to buy things—they feel entitled to own you, too. You are there to serve them and if you don't understand their foolish questions, meet their insane demands, or give them what they want, they'll take it out on you. Have you ever tried changing a diaper with mittens on or coaxing a child using only Brussels sprouts? Both are easier than making a customer happy.

AT WORK TODAY, I HAD A CUSTOMER ASK ME TO OPEN A HOUSE LOCK, SINCE I AM A LOCKSMITH. I ASKED HER HOW LONG THEY'D LIVED IN THE HOUSE. "UH," SHE SAID AND FROWNED, "IS THAT A REQUIREMENT?" I'M DUMBEMPLOYED.

Tip

Great waiters can anticipate what a diner wants, so don't bother asking for their order.

At work today, I took dictation for a lawyer at our firm. That was fine, and he's pretty polite. At the end, though, he asked me to stay fifteen minutes longer. I proceeded to record the text of his dictated poetry. He tried to rhyme words with "orange." I'm dumbemployed.

At work today, I was selling Halloween candy to a few people. They asked me if there was something cheaper than candy corn. I know which house to skip. I'm dumbemployed.

At work today, I had to ask an old lady to stop feeding the pigeons near my pretzel cart. "It's a free country!" she shouted. She then laid down a path of breadcrumbs around my cart. I got pigeon-bombed. I'm dumbemployed.

DOES A CUSTOMER NEED HELP?

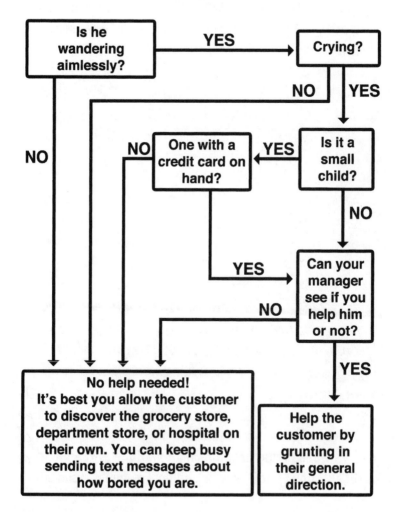

At work today, I had a patient who told me about her childhood. I'm a therapist, so it's my job to listen. But shouldn't the most boring childhood ever have been less traumatizing? I'm dumbemployed.

At work today, I had a lady hand me three different coupons, all of which were expired. She then went on a five-minute rant against me. Total value of the coupons? $1.34. I'm dumbemployed.

AT WORK TODAY, A VERY STURDY-LOOKING RUSSIAN MAN CAME INTO OUR COFFEE SHOP. "VODKA," HE SAID. THE BEST I COULD OFFER HIM WAS A STRONG GLASS OF ORANGE JUICE. I'M DUMBEMPLOYED.

At work today, my wife and I were stocking shelves at our craft store. Three teenagers came in and asked us for "mom gifts." Then they complained that we didn't have any video games. Is that what their moms want? I'm dumbemployed.

At work today, I had a customer ask me if plasma TVs were made from plasma donations at the blood bank. I don't think he was kidding. I'm dumbemployed.

AT WORK TODAY, I WROTE E=MC^2 ON THE CHALKBOARD TO MAKE A POINT TO MY CLASS ABOUT INVENTION. INSTEAD, I SPENT TWENTY MINUTES EXPLAINING WHY THE 2 WAS SO TINY. THAT'S WHAT I GET FOR TEACHING EINSTEIN TO FOURTH-GRADERS. I'M DUMBEMPLOYED.

At work today, I had a woman ask me to give her a special haircut that looked "frilly but not too busy, cute but mature, and happy but serious." I just took off an inch and she was happy. I'm dumbemployed.

Tip

Got a customer complaint? Distract them with a coupon, free give-away, or fire.

At work today, I sold a cat scratching post at our pet store. After I handed the customer his receipt, he asked me if catnip worked on humans. I'm dumbemployed.

At work today, I served shots to three coeds. They were laughing and giggling and, I thought, flirting. Then they asked me what it was like to be from "an earlier generation." I'm dumbemployed.

At work today, I had three students come up to me after class with a petition labeled "The No Homework Petition." Kids, I may teach democracy, but this classroom isn't one. I'm dumbemployed.

At work today, I got to put three items on discount. All three were items I'd bought with my employee discount. That means I have bad timing and bad taste. I'm dumbemployed.

AT WORK TODAY, I SERVED LUNCH TO MY USUAL GANG OF FOURTH-GRADERS. I'M NOT A NUTRITIONIST, BUT SOMETHING TELLS ME IT'S NOT GOOD WHEN SOMEBODY EATS A DIET CONSISTING ENTIRELY OF TATER TOTS. I'M DUMBEMPLOYED.

At work today, I had a guy come into the store and ask me to help him choose throw pillows. I asked him what he wanted. "Something girly," he said. Is there a masculine throw pillow? I'm dumbemployed.

AT WORK TODAY, IT WAS RAINING VERY HEAVILY. I COLLECTED UMBRELLAS AT THE FRONT. I THOUGHT I WAS DOING A GREAT JOB, UNTIL I WAS INFORMED I'D GIVEN A $220 UMBRELLA TO THE WRONG PERSON. I'M DUMBEMPLOYED.

At work today, I saw one middle-aged woman buying blueberries three times. The third time, I asked her why she'd come back. "Can you make a blueberry pie?" she asked me. I think she was serious. I'm dumbemployed.

At work today, two customers were discussing American Idol. By the end of the conversation, both agreed they could do better than the contestants—which I would believe if their combined age had been less than one hundred. I'm dumbemployed.

At work today, I believed I was about to make a sale to a client. Turns out he was just pumping me for prices. That's normal. The bad part is that I gave him every price he needed. I'm dumbemployed.

tip

Shoplifters have gotten cleverer over the years. Remember that full body cavity searches can be useful tools to prevent theft.

At work today, I didn't have time to shave. I had one customer ask me if I was a pirate. I wish I hadn't left my eye patch at home. I'm dumbemployed.

At work today, I was working as a teller. A customer asked me for a certain amount "in quarters only." He wanted $6.35. I'm dumbemployed.

At work today, I had a student in my advanced grammar course at my college ask me a question. His question was when to use "who" versus "what." "Whom" is reserved for the second advanced course, I guess. I'm dumbemployed.

AT WORK TODAY, I WAS TELLING A CUSTOMER ABOUT A PLASMA TV. THE USUAL STUFF. THEN SHE ASKED ME IF IT PLAYED "CURSE WORDS." I JUST TOLD HER NO—IT'S EASIER THAT WAY. I'M DUMBEMPLOYED.

At work today, a pair of girls who couldn't have been over fifteen tried to buy cigarettes. Here's a tip, girls: don't show me your high school student IDs when I ask for identification. I'm dumbemployed.

At work today, I was supposed to clean bathrooms. As I went in, a customer exited and smiled at me. "You can see my masterpiece," he said. Then I did. I'm dumbemployed.

At work today, I had to break up a fight. It wasn't between two customers. It was between a customer and a mannequin. I wasn't sure whose side to take. I'm dumbemployed.

At work today, I pretended I was British for about three customers. It was a dare, and it went well—until somebody from the UK showed up. He walked out of the store after about thirty seconds of it. I'm dumbemployed.

The customer is always right, unless they ask you to steal something.

At work today, a group of cheerleaders at the school I work at were parading around in black tights that were far too revealing. "We're cats," one of them told me. Last time I checked, cats didn't have midriffs. I'm dumbemployed.

AT WORK TODAY, I CALLED A BINGO GAME AT THE ELDERLY HOME WHERE I WORK. I THOUGHT I'D HAVE TO WORK ON FIGURING OUT WHO WON. INSTEAD, I ENDED UP BREAKING UP TWO FIGHTS. I'M DUMBEMPLOYED.

At work today, I had a father come into our children's clothing store. I asked him what he wanted. "Clothes." I asked him what size and he shrugged. "A girl?" he asked. A girl is not a size, sir. I'm dumbemployed.

At work today, I gave a long museum tour to a fourth-grade class. I worked my little heart out— accents, voices, demonstrations, and everything. When it was done, I got only one question: "Where's the bathroom?" I'm dumbemployed.

Tip

If a customer pays with a credit card, save the numbers for later so you can buy them anything you think they might want.

AT WORK TODAY, A CUSTOMER BOUGHT A FOUR-PACK OF DVDS AND ASKED ME IF THEY WOULD HOLD HOLLYWOOD MOVIES. I THEN GAVE INSTRUCTIONS ON HOW TO ILLEGALLY COPY MOVIES WHILE BEING PAID $6.85 AN HOUR TO DO IT. I'M DUMBEMPLOYED.

At work today, I had to give a lady a really top shelf prime rib. She asked if the cow it came from was "free range." I handed her the meat and told her that it's nothing now—it's dead. She told my manager and now I'm on probation. I'm dumbemployed.

AT WORK TODAY, I SENT AN EMAIL TO MY MOM ABOUT MY DAD'S RECENT KIDNEY STONE ORDEAL. I DETAILED SOME OF THE GRAPHIC ISSUES. AND THEN I REALIZED I'D ACTUALLY SENT IT TO A CLIENT WITH MY MOM'S FIRST NAME. I'M DUMB-EMPLOYED.

At work today, I gave horseback-riding lessons to a boy who is apparently the son of a CEO. After nearly being bucked off twice, he wrinkled his face and looked at me before asking if he could delegate his horseback-riding responsibilities. I'm dumbemployed.

At work today, I was working at a family apple orchard. A middle-aged woman came up in a limousine and asked me if the apples were organic or not. Except that she didn't say organic. I'd never heard of orgasmic apples before. I'm dumbemployed.

At work today, a bald man came into our store and asked for three baseball caps. Later on, he told me he needed something to wear to a wedding that weekend. I didn't have the heart to tell him that people would still figure out what had happened to his hair. I'm dumbemployed.

At work today, I had a parent call in with a complaint about her child's treatment in my cooking class. The parent thought her kid was being left out. I then reminded the parent that her child didn't show up to class today. I'm dumbemployed.

Tip

When recommending clothing to a customer, never admit to them how fat they are.

AT WORK TODAY, I HAD A SCRUFFY GOATEED GUY COME INTO OUR DEALERSHIP LOOKING TO OFFER US A TRADE-IN. HE WAS OFFERING A VESPA SCOOTER, A MICROWAVE, AND A NINTENDO WII. WE'RE A CAR DEALERSHIP, SON, NOT A PAWNSHOP. I'M DUMBEMPLOYED.

At work today, I received a twenty-minute lecture from a client. He shouted at me that I needed to work on my "intrapurposeful skills." It took me that long to realize he was talking about interpersonal skills. I'm dumbemployed.

At work today, two customers got into a fight. That's typical at a bar, I guess. But I work at a toy store. That's what a hot toy will do to parents. I'm dumbemployed.

At work today, a plumber came into our hardware store asking for tape. I asked him what he needed. "Something cheaper than the pipe I should get, but still strong." Duct tape really does do everything, I guess. I'm dumbemployed.

At work today, a foreign customer came into the store looking for shoes. It took me twenty minutes to verify that she was actually looking for a computer. She still bought $300 in heels. I'm dumbemployed.

AT WORK TODAY, I VIEWED A TRAINING VIDEO FOR MY JOB AS A CASHIER. A DIRECT QUOTE FROM THE VIDEO TOLD US THAT MANY OF OUR CUSTOMERS WOULD BE IRASCIBLE, ANGRY, OR UPSET. AFTER I WATCHED IT, SOMEBODY TOLD ME THAT THE TRAINING VIDEO REALLY SUGARCOATS THINGS. I'M DUMBEMPLOYED.

At work today, I guided a very young teen to some parenting books. I couldn't help asking him why he needed them, and he muttered that he'd heard making babies was fun. I took him to a different section. I'm dumbemployed.

AT WORK TODAY, WE HAD A TOWN HALL MEETING AND I GOT TO MODERATE THE QUESTIONS. DID YOU KNOW THAT OUR TOWNSPEOPLE HAVE VERY STRONG OPINIONS ABOUT PAPER TOILET SEAT COVERS IN THE PUBLIC LIBRARY? I'M DUMBEMPLOYED.

Tip

If you're worried about losing an important client, try using handcuffs.

At work today, a customer yelled at me for being ignorant. I work at a gym and he handed me an ID, insisting on admission. He was a white guy who was balding. The guy on the ID was Asian with a full head of hair. I'm dumbemployed.

At work today, I had the honor of waiting tables at a sorority event. I was actually told by someone named Kelli to work a little faster. I think she'd forgotten that we're in the same English discussion group. I'm dumbemployed.

At work today, I was assigned to police the movie theater for jerks on their cell phone. I found one five minutes in who claimed it was his First Amendment right to talk as loud as he wants. I'm dumbemployed.

At work today, I was cleaning out the demo appliance units. Apparently, customers view them as trashcans. One fridge contained three empty soda cans. And one full one. I'm dumbemployed.

AT WORK TODAY, I WAS GIVING DANCE LESSONS TO A VERY OLD COUPLE THAT WANTED TO LEARN THE SALSA. I'M ALL FOR CONTINUING EDUCATION. BUT WHEN WALKING HURTS YOUR BACK, YOU PROBABLY SHOULD LOOK SOMEWHERE LESS PAINFUL FOR LOVE. I'M DUMBEMPLOYED.

At work today, I kept getting distracted by a beautiful woman shopping in our thrift store. It was a good thing, really—because I was watching her so closely, I easily saw her shoplift three items. My heart was broken. I'm dumbemployed.

At work today, I showed a house that was completely empty. The woman seeing it asked me if the biggest room was a living room or a dining room. I don't think she understands that the owner gets to choose. I'm dumbemployed.

How YOU ARE TAKING CARE OF BUSINESS, ACCORDING TO BACHMAN-TURNER OVERDRIVE

EVERY DAY

EVERY WAY

WORKING OVERTIME

IT'S ALL MINE

At work today, a cowboy-type came into the store and asked me if we sold Wrangler jeans. That's a reasonable question in a clothing store. But not in a hardware store. I'm dumbemployed.

AT WORK TODAY, I COULDN'T LET A CUSTOMER RETURN A TELEVISION THAT HE'D MANAGED TO SPILL ORANGE JUICE ON. IT'S THE COMPANY RULES. BUT HE STILL THREATENED ME WITH A "SWIFT REPRISAL." APPARENTLY, I JUST BECAME A SUPERVILLAIN'S ENEMY. I'M DUMBEMPLOYED.

At work today, the mower got stuck on a big old rock. I stopped it, which was good, because I then saw that a toddler had been chasing after me. The parents waved to me with smiles on their faces, oblivious. I'm dumbemployed.

At work today, a mother came in with her kid and the nanny, whom I recognize from other days at the café. The mom said that the kid wanted a cookie. I asked what type. The mom didn't know the answer, but the nanny did. I'm dumbemployed.

AT WORK TODAY, A NOTABLE LOCAL CELEBRITY CAME INTO OUR STORE AND BOUGHT A CARTON OF CIGARETTES AND ANOTHER CARTON OF TEETH WHITENER. HE SLIPPED ME $5 TO "KEEP IT UNDER MY HAT." IT'S THE BEST TIP I'LL EVER GET. I'M DUMBEMPLOYED.

Tip

A good salesman makes the customer feel smart, so grunt and run into walls as often as possible.

At work today, my register was telling me that a customer had a negative account balance, so I couldn't sell him anything. The awkward conversation ended with tears, blushing, and a promise to do better. The customer was a forty-year-old man with a mustache. I'm dumbemployed.

AT WORK TODAY, IT WAS "NEW MOM DAY" AT OUR BOOKSTORE, WHERE WE GAVE A LECTURE WITH A MATERNITY AUTHOR. HAVE YOU EVER TRIED TO MEDIATE A STROLLER TRAFFIC JAM? THEY HAVE ROAD RAGE, TOO. I'M DUMBEMPLOYED.

At work today, I had a customer ask me for vodka bottle service. Our bar's most expensive drink is a $4 beer. I'm dumbemployed.

At work today, I was pushing against a deadline with a customer who needed a slogan for their housecleaning service. Do you think they'll like "We suck, vacuum style"? That's what I thought. I'm dumbemployed.

At work today, a hipster-type girl came into the record store and started flirting with me. But then she asked for Justin Bieber. Never have I fallen out of love so quickly. I'm dumbemployed.

At work today, a couple of people came in on a motor-cycle looking to buy our rather expensive scarves. They bought two wool ones, put them on, and rode away into the rain, quickly ruining them. Another day's work. I'm dumbemployed.

tip

Avoid fighting. A customer with a bloody nose is rarely a repeat customer.

At work today, I had a customer call me about his investment portfolio. He demanded to sell all his stocks immediately. I then reminded him he doesn't own any. He was still mad at me. I'm dumbemployed.

AT WORK TODAY, I CAUGHT ONE OF OUR CUSTOMERS IN THE BATHROOM SHAVING. THAT'S WEIRD ENOUGH. BUT HE WAS SHAVING HIS HEAD. I JUST LEFT AS QUICKLY AS I COULD. I'M DUMBEMPLOYED.

Tip

Unusual window signs can attract new customers, especially if they feature nudity.

At work today, our zoo tour group was really crowded with kids and parents. I tended to one kid who cried because he didn't get to touch the lion. His dad sided with him instead of me. I'm dumbemployed.

At work today, a Russian man entered our appliance store and asked for a "wacuum." It took me three times to understand that he wanted a vacuum. I'm dumbemployed.

At work today, I had a customer ask me for the "new" Jimi Hendrix record. I'm dumbemployed.

At work today, a group of nerds came into the sporting-goods store. They were looking to buy foam swords to simulate medieval warfare. All I could offer them was a football helmet. I'm dumbemployed.

At work today, some teenagers were trying to do Parkour outside our store. I got to call the ambulance twice. I'm dumbemployed.

At work today, I offered a customer a sample of our patented fried Twinkies. She asked me if it was organic. I'm dumbemployed.

At work today, we were all dressed up in Halloween costumes to give a bit of fun to our customers. Our most vocal response was a crying two-year-old. I'm dumbemployed.

At work today, a female customer came into our lingerie store looking for our smallest sizes. Apparently, she thought her nine-year-old needed to get something more sophisticated. I'm dumbemployed.

At work today, a lady came into our pet store and asked for a dog that was guaranteed not to eat her toddler. I said, "I'm sorry miss, we only sell dogs that eat babies." She left in a huff. I'm dumbemployed.

At work today, a family ate at our restaurant and their four-year-old cried. I asked if he might want a pacifier. He said he wouldn't stop unless he got a sundae. It was nine a.m. I'm dumbemployed.

At work today, I was consulting a potential client on his health insurance plan. He didn't listen to my recommendation for deductibles and co-pays. He wanted something that would make him thinner. I'm dumbemployed.

Tip

Snagging a customer is like trying to get a date. Play hard to get and hide as long as possible. They'll love it!

At work today, a customer came to my deli counter shouting that it would take forever for me to call his number, which was 91. I then pointed out to him that he was holding it up-side-down. I'm dumbemployed.

AT WORK TODAY, A PREGNANT WOMAN CAME INTO OUR STORE TO BUY CHAMPAGNE. I MADE A JOKE ABOUT HER DRINKING ALCOHOL. "YEAH," SHE SAID, "THANK GOODNESS CHAMPAGNE DOESN'T HAVE ANY ALCO-HOL IN IT." I'M DUMBEMPLOYED.

At work today, I wore a flannel shirt. Not a good idea, since I sell electronics to less-than-hip middle-aged people. I got asked all day if I was a lumberjack. I'm dumbemployed.

At work today, I sold a graphic video game to a twelve-year-old boy. I had no choice, due to our policies. The look in his eyes said, "I'm ready to be scarred for life." I'm dumbemployed.

AT WORK TODAY, I WAS HELPING A CUSTOMER UPGRADE HIS CELL PHONE WHEN SOMEBODY PAGED HIM. YES, HE HAD A PAGER. I CAN SEE WHY HE WANTED TO UPGRADE. I'M DUMBEMPLOYED.

Tip

To sell well, you have to believe in the product. That's a top argument for selling only products that actually exist.

At work today, I caught an eleven-year-old boy looking at a copy of *Playboy*. It's packaged in plastic wrap, but he kept rubbing the edge, like he could wish it away. I'm dumbemployed.

At work today, I had a customer literally beg me for a discount. When I say literally, I mean that he got down on his knees and shook his hands. The discount ended up being 10 percent and a free bucket hat. I'm dumbemployed.

At work today, two customers came into the hardware store and spent the entire time arguing about sports. I'd make more money here if I could take bets. I'm dumbemployed.

At work today, I had to extract a tooth, which is never very fun. After I yanked it out, my patient asked me if I could do the same to a hangnail he had. I'm dumbemployed.

At work today, I showed a client a design for their new guesthouse. They said it was too homey. I wasn't aware that was a bad thing. But I still lost the job. I'm dumbemployed.

AT WORK TODAY, I TRIED TO REASON WITH A CUSTOMER WHO WANTED A 50 PERCENT DISCOUNT ON A USED CAR. I GAVE HIM A FREE DVD PLAYER AND HE CAME UP $3,000 ON THE PRICE. I'M DUMBEMPLOYED.

At work today, I had a customer ask which soap would "clean him goodest." I'm dumbemployed.

At work today, a customer with a broken nose came in. He was a regular, so I asked him how he did it. He told me that it wasn't any of my business. Turns out he was right—my coworker did it in a bar. I'm dumbemployed.

Giving a customer a product you know is broken? Call it a "beta" and they'll thank you for the opportunity.

At work today, the food in our meat case was spoiling, so we marked it down. A customer saw it and asked me if she still had to cook it. I'm dumbemployed.

At work today, I had a customer ask me which escalator was the up escalator. Both of them were clearly in view. I'm dumbemployed.

At work today, I told a customer she could remember our phone number through a mnemonic device. She slapped me and told me my "sexual comments" were inappropriate. I'm dumbemployed.

At work today, one customer displayed the essence of my job. I sold her an apricot which, a minute later, she tried to return for not being ripe enough. I'm dumbemployed.

At work today, I gave a customer my phone number for emergencies only. Somehow, we've already exchanged six text messages. I'm dumbemployed.

Tip

You should have fresh breath when speaking to a client, so have mouthwash in your mouth at all times.

At work today, I had a single stick of beef jerky during my break. For the rest of the day, customers were asking me what had died inside the store. I'll stick to apples from now on. I'm dumbemployed.

At work today, I found a phone in the dressing room. I called the number that said "Mom." Whoever it was, they didn't recognize the number. I'm dumbemployed.

AT WORK TODAY, A CUSTOMER ASKED ME FOR A RECOMMENDATION ON TYPES OF CANDY A FOUR-YEAR-OLD BOY WOULD LIKE. IS THERE ANY HE WOULDN'T? I'M DUMBEMPLOYED.

TALKING TO CUSTOMERS

- Try to make a good impression—De Niro is easy if you can't do any others.

- Address all your customers as sir or madam. When in doubt, alternate between the two.

- Anticipate the customer's order. "You look depressed! Can I get you another appletini?"

- Go for the upsell. If you're in life insurance, try suggesting that it's likely all of their family members will die.

- Use the customer's name to indicate familiarity. If you've forgotten their name, just time a sneeze each time you say it.

- No customer wants to be talked to like a child. Treat them like they're at least thirteen.

At work today, we let a tiny bit of sun into the showroom. It was nice, until a customer howled that it might slightly lighten the furniture upholstery. I'm dumbemployed.

At work today, I discovered a customer camped out in front of our store at six in the morning, because he wanted to beat the line for that day's new comic book release. We open at ten. I'm dumbemployed.

At work today, we had a whole set of misprinted coupons. Try telling a customer that their 100 percent off coupon is actually only for 10 percent. I'm dumbemployed.

At work today, I asked a customer if he preferred an acoustic or electric guitar. He asked which one would sound more like Hendrix. No, he didn't know the answer on his own. I'm dumbemployed.

AT WORK TODAY, A CUSTOMER ASKED ME TO PROVIDE AN OBJECTIVE OPINION IN A DISPUTE WITH HIS WIFE. SOMEHOW, I HAD BOTH OF THEM HATING ME BY THE END. I'M DUMBEMPLOYED.

AT WORK TODAY, I SHOWED UP AFTER EXERCISING. MY FIRST CUSTOMER ASKED ME IF I NEEDED A DOCTOR. I'M DUMBEMPLOYED.

At work today, a customer bought camping gear and asked me if there were any bears in the area. We're in Texas. Anybody who doesn't know the answer shouldn't be camping. I'm dumbemployed.

AT WORK TODAY, I TRIED TO ESCAPE THE FLOOR FOR A QUICK BREAK, SO I DUCKED THROUGH THE BACK DOOR. OUTSIDE, CUSTOMERS WERE WAITING FOR ME ANYWAY. I'M DUMBEMPLOYED.

At work today, I had to get a colonoscopy at lunch. I saw a client in the waiting room, and he punched me on the shoulder. "Looks like you'll be getting exactly what you do to your customers." I think he was right. I'm dumbemployed.

At work today, a teenager came into our store and bought three posters of the human anatomy. He informed me he was going to sell them on the black market at his middle school. I'm dumbemployed.

At work today, a customer asked me if there was a device like a remote control, but for a treadmill. Can you really run on a treadmill from across the room? I'm dumbemployed.

Tip

Giving your customers recommendations on food can be useful, but don't tell them they should go on a diet.

At work today, an old woman complained that the movie theater was too cold. She was wearing a heavy coat, a hat, and a scarf. At what point do you realize that it may just be your body? I'm dumbemployed.

At work today, I was talking to a potential client when she said "footnote" before clarifying her comment. I've decided that I'm talking to the wrong types of people. I'm dumbemployed.

At work today, a customer wore headphones during his entire meal. I thought the point of headphones was to keep music private. Instead, we all heard his reggae for an hour. I'm dumbemployed.

AT WORK TODAY, I ASKED A POSSIBLE BUSINESS PARTNER IF HE WAS INTERESTED IN GRABBING A MEAL. HE SUGGESTED A STRIP CLUB. I'M DUMBEMPLOYED.

At work today, I was building cabinets for a client who wanted something "homey, but corporate." I'm dumbemployed.

Keep the consumer happy with coupons that don't expire for at least an hour.

At work today, a client asked me if we were open on weekends. When I told him we weren't, he laughed. "You are now," he said. I'm dumbemployed.

At work today, some old women shopping at our store were giggling. Apparently, they thought my manager was a hottie. He's only sixty-five. I'm dumbemployed.

At work today, I let the stress of my job get to me when I shouted at a client on the phone. I apologized for a pretty long time and waited for an answer. Then I realized he'd already hung up. I'm dumbemployed.

At work today, a very slight man came into our gym and said he wanted to take boxing lessons. I asked him if he was a beginner. "I don't know," he said. "I play a lot of boxing video games." I'm dumbemployed.

Clients love to be wined and dined, so make sure you take them to a McDonald's that allows alcohol inside.

At work today, a customer asked me if she could pay with an IOU. I work at a Best Buy. I'm dumbemployed.

AT WORK TODAY, I HAD A CUSTOMER REQUEST THAT I CUT HIS PIZZA—INTO INDIVIDUAL SQUARE-INCH BITES. I'M DUMBEMPLOYED.

At work today, somebody came to the drive-thru with an open twelve-pack of beer in the passenger seat. I'm dumbemployed.

At work today, I sold a balloon to a child. She immediately cast the string into the air. "I had to free it," she said. My first thought was that it was good advertising. I'm dumbemployed.

THE PEOPLE YOU MEET AT WORK

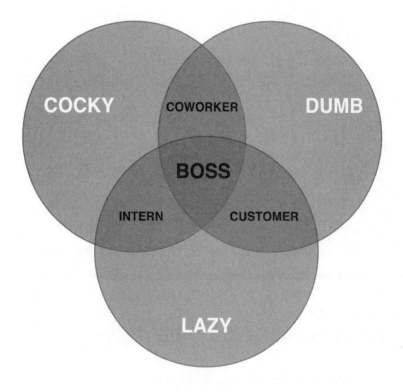

At work today, I installed cable TV into a customer's home. Here's a thought: before the cable guy comes over, you should probably put away your giant lit bong. I'm dumbemployed.

At work today, we had somebody ask for a vegan cake. That's fine, except for the fact that I work for a drugstore. Before serving vegan food, we need to get actual food first. I'm dumbemployed.

At work today, I had two customers ask for shots of coke instead of vodka. They weren't former alcoholics or anything—they just wanted to save money. Bottoms up. I'm dumbemployed.

At work today, I had an old guy say he had the most satisfying meal he'd ever had at our restaurant. All he'd had was a grilled cheese sandwich. "Not even you," he said, "could screw that up." I'm dumbemployed.

AT WORK TODAY, THEY TOLD US OUR BUDGET SURPLUS WOULD BE SPENT ON CUSTOMER CARE. I WORK AT A GYM. WE'RE GIVING THEM CHOCOLATES AT THE DOOR. I'M DUMBEMPLOYED.

At work today, a customer called our restaurant and asked if our lunch buffet was available for delivery. I'm dumbemployed.

At work today, our theater manager told us we needed to sparkle at the ticket counter. Unfortunately, he meant it literally and had the glitter to enforce it. I'm dumbemployed.

AT WORK TODAY, I SOLD A CUSTOMER A FAKE MUSTACHE. "COSTUME PARTY?" I ASKED. "MIND YOUR OWN BUSINESS," HE REPLIED. I'M DUMBEMPLOYED.

Customers can be kept happy through great service and a steady supply of nitrous oxide in the ventilation system.

At work today, a guy bought six cement blocks. I asked him if he needed delivery help, and he said no. He then proceeded to pile the bricks into his leather-upholstered convertible. Ouch. I'm dumbemployed.

At work today, a customer asked when we were open. "Every weekday," I told her. She looked at me. "So you're open Saturday?" I'm dumbemployed.

At work today, I sold a fur coat to a very young woman. I asked casually how she would be paying for it. She then proceeded to pour paint on it and run out the door. I'm dumbemployed.

At work today, a lady came into the office lobby and asked me what the weather was like. She was just outside. Shouldn't she know? I'm dumbemployed.

At work today, I sold a customer lettuce and soy sauce and casually asked what she was making. "Dinner." I asked her what else was in her meal. "This is all," she said. I'm dumbemployed.

AT WORK TODAY, I THOUGHT WE'D TRY A NEW SHADE OF MAKEUP ON ONE OF MY MOST LOYAL CUSTOMERS. SHE'S SET, AS LONG AS SHE'S AUDITIONING TO BE A CLOWN. I'M DUMBEMPLOYED.

At work today, I was asked if I could bring out a plate of ketchup because the bottle was too slow. I'm dumbemployed.

AT WORK TODAY, I WAS WORKING THE SECTION OF OUR STORE WITH ALL THE TV SETS. THAT WAS WHEN I SAW AN EIGHT-YEAR-OLD SHOVE A REMOTE CONTROL INTO HIS PANTS. IT MIGHT BE SHOPLIFTING—BUT I DON'T WANT THE REMOTE BACK. I'M DUMBEMPLOYED.

At work today, a man called for our catering services and asked if we could deliver to his boat, which was in the middle of Lake Michigan when he called. I'm dumbemployed.

At work today, a customer asked if he could use our copy machine, which is located in a back room. I later walked in on him making an important Xerox of his butt. I'm dumbemployed.

At work today, a caller wanted to cancel her magazine subscription. We're required to ask why, and the answer was that "reading's too hard these days." I'm dumbemployed.

AT WORK TODAY, SOMEBODY CAME INTO THE STORE AND ASKED IF WE HAD HIGH HEELS. I TOLD HIM WE PROBABLY DIDN'T HAVE HEELS IN HIS SIZE. I'M DUMBEMPLOYED.

Tip

Customers hate stale bread, so don't let them see the expiration date was a month ago.

At work today, I was finishing up a table. I work at a pretty nice restaurant, so usually customers order an after-dinner drink. I asked this guy if I could get him anything. He smiled. "I'd love a McFlurry." He was serious. My manager made me go across the street and get it. I'm dumbemployed.

At work today, when I finished my lecture, a student came up to talk to me. "My knee hurts," he said. I asked him what he wanted me to do about it. "Aren't you a doctor?" he asked. I am a doctor. My doctorate is in Renaissance Literature. I'm dumbemployed.

At work today, a teenage goth-type girl came into our store. I was worried she was going to shoplift, so I asked her if she needed anything. I work at a pet store. She wanted a dog collar. For herself. I found her one that fit. I'm dumbemployed.

WHAT YOUR CUSTOMERS WANT

I need a new refrigerator, but I want one that makes things warm, too.

I need a car that has great miles per gallon and is easy to park. Also, it should be an SUV.

Can you make me a new deck that has carpet, a roof, walls, and central air?

I really love your art, but can it be less abstract and involve a lot more unicorns?

At work today, we got a call from an international telemarketer. "Hello, is this One H Zero P?" I work at an IHOP. I'm dumbemployed.

At work today, I was driving a couple of really blonde girls to a bar. Really blonde. They opened their windows and started high-fiving everybody. Then one person held on to the girl's hand. I kept driving. She dislocated her shoulder. I'm dumbemployed.

AT WORK TODAY, I WAS SELLING TICKETS FOR AN UP-COMING SHOW AND THIS WOMAN CAME UP TO ME AND ASKED, "HOW MUCH IS THE $12 TICKET?" I REPLIED NICELY AND SAID, "$12." I'M DUMBEMPLOYED.

Tip

Never swear in front of a customer. Always wait until you can do it behind their back.

At work today, a lady came to the concierge desk and asked where the closest Bank of America was because she didn't want to pay the $2 surcharge at the ATM in-house. It's two miles away, which makes it a $10 cab ride. She took the cab. I'm dumbemployed.

At work today, a young woman came into the store. She said she was looking for a hemp bag. She bought that— and a lighter. She left with a big grin. I didn't have the heart to tell her that hemp doesn't work like that. I'm dumbemployed.

At work today, a couple of clients were waiting in reception. We have rolly chairs there. I shouldn't have looked away. When I looked back, one was pushing the other in circles. And these people rank higher than I *do*. I'm dumbemployed.

AT WORK TODAY, I INSPECTED A HOUSE ABOUT TO GO ON THE MARKET. THE WIFE WAS THE ONLY ONE THERE. THEY HAD TERMITES. THE WIFE ASKED ME IF THAT WAS BAD. THEIR HOUSE IS MADE ALMOST ENTIRELY OF WOOD. I'M DUMBEMPLOYED.

At work today, I had a customer sit in a chair that's supposed to help his back. He came back two hours later and handed me a chiropractor's bill. "This is your fault," he said. I'm dumbemployed.

AT WORK TODAY, A TEENAGER CAME INTO THE DRUG-STORE WITH A JAR FULL OF PENNIES. HE POURED THEM ON THE TABLE AND ASKED FOR CIGARETTES. THEN I ID'D HIM. IT TOOK HIM FIVE MINUTES TO PUT ALL THE PENNIES BACK IN HIS JAR. I'M DUMBEMPLOYED.

Tip

If a customer wants to know where your products are manufactured, let them know that your company uses only ethical labor. That lie usually works.

At work today, the customers were weirder than usual. I refold clothes when customers mess them up. It's boring but fine. Today I caught one customer going through the stacks and refolding them all herself. She said her kids were all grown up and she missed their laundry. I'm dumbemployed.

At work today, I applied a nice thick coat of varnish to a table we're making for a customer. I showed it to him and, for some reason, he touched it. "I don't know," he said. "I don't want my table to always be wet." Sir, varnish dries. I'm dumbemployed.

YOUR TURN!

At work today, _____

_____

_____

_____

_____

_____

_____

_____

_____I'm dumbemployed.

At work today, _____

_____

_____

_____

_____

_____

_____

_____I'm dumbemployed.

At work today, _____

_____

_____

_____

_____

_____

_____

_____

_____I'm dumbemployed.

At work today, _____

_____

_____

_____

_____

_____

_____

_____I'm dumbemployed.

At work today, _____
_____
_____
_____
_____
_____
_____
_____
_____
_____I'm dumbemployed.

At work today, _____
_____
_____
_____
_____
_____
_____
_____
_____I'm dumbemployed.

At work today, _____

_____

_____

_____

_____

_____

_____

_____

_____I'm dumbemployed.

At work today, _____

_____

_____

_____

_____

_____

_____

_____I'm dumbemployed.

At work today, _____
_____
_____
_____
_____
_____
_____
_____
_____I'm dumbemployed.

At work today, _____
_____
_____
_____
_____
_____
_____
_____
_____I'm dumbemployed.

JUST DUMB

Work can be like a series of hangnails that refuse to come off, a splinter stuck stubbornly in your foot, or a popcorn kernel wedged in between your back teeth. You deal with so many things at work that it gets to a point when you hardly even notice them anymore. From the minor irritations to major screw-ups, the only thing consistent in your work life is that whatever happens will probably be dumb.

At work today, a student of mine requested a sticker for his homework about butterflies. He started crying when I refused. That would be reasonable—if he'd actually written anything on the paper. I'm dumbemployed.

At work today, I was folding shirts when a customer tapped me on the shoulder. "Do you have any W-neck shirts?" he asked. I don't want to know what that looks like. I'm dumbemployed.

Tip

You can improve your water cooler small talk by practicing at night. Stake out a top spot near your bathtub and start chatting!

AT WORK TODAY, I RECEIVED A REFUND REQUEST FOR A GUITAR. THE CUSTOMER'S REASON WAS THAT IT DIDN'T "PLAY GOOD ENOUGH." I HAD HIM PLAY SOME IN-STORE MODELS AFTER THAT. TRUST ME—IT WASN'T THE GUITAR'S FAULT THAT IT DIDN'T PLAY GOOD ENOUGH. I'M DUMBEMPLOYED.

At work today, I received a reservation request for a honeymoon suite with two beds. Some honeymoon. I'm dumbemployed.

At work today, I parked my car in the special employee lot. That means I had to walk over a bridge, underneath a dripping air conditioner, and through a long back hallway to actually get to work. I'm dumbemployed.

At work today, I gave jet ski lessons to a couple with an infant. They tried to strap the baby on the back until I told them it wouldn't be safe. The guy cursed me out. I'm dumbemployed.

AT WORK TODAY, A PERSON WHO LIVES IN MY BUILDING ASKED ME IF I LIKED BEING A DOORMAN. I TOLD HIM I WAS DOING IT TO SUPPORT MYSELF THROUGH COLLEGE. HE ASKED ME WHY A DOORMAN WOULD NEED A COLLEGE DEGREE. I'M DUMBEMPLOYED.

At work today, I was staffing the furniture section. Then my coworker volunteered to take it from me. I asked him why. "Somebody's got to patrol for bedbugs." I'm dumbemployed.

At work today, my office celebrated casual Friday. For the event, I wore a polo shirt and shorts. Only halfway through did I find out that the rest of the office had interpreted "casual Friday" as "take Friday off day." I'm dumbemployed.

CIGARETTE BREAK ETIQUETTE

- Offer your coworkers a light. If they are under eighteen, offer them cigarettes, since they can't buy them on their own and will feel left out.

- If you haven't had enough, combine your two fifteen-minute breaks into one thirty-minute session. Your boss will understand.

- Roll your own tobacco from your coworkers' butts. It will help you connect with your team.

- To save time, fit two cigarettes in your mouth so you can get back to work more quickly.

- If possible, put cigarette purchases on a corporate account. They increase productivity and keep you from attacking your coworkers.

At work today, I found myself preparing a document for a judge. Sounds fancy, right? It was a lunch menu. I'm dumbemployed.

At work today, I gave tennis lessons to the superintendent's wife. She spent the entire time dishing about lawsuits against the district—where my son is a student. I had to just smile the whole time. I'm dumbemployed.

AT WORK TODAY, THERE WERE ABOUT TWENTY NEW CUSTOMERS WHO CAME IN DUE TO AN AD IN THE NEWSPAPER. THE AD PROMISED A TOY FOR HALF OFF. OF COURSE, WE ONLY HAD FOUR TOYS. I HAD TO FEND OFF THE ANGRY CUSTOMERS. I'M DUMBEMPLOYED.

At work today, I spilled at least half a cup of coffee on my blouse. I walked around self-conscious the whole day—but nobody even noticed until 4:45. I guess I make that much of an impression. I'm dumbemployed.

At work today, my coworker came in with three shirt buttons unbuttoned. That's three too many. I had a chest hair matinee. I'm dumbemployed.

At work today, I sold a collectible 1964 baseball card. As it left the building, I realized that I've become a little too committed to my work: I was crying. It's bad when business success makes you depressed. I'm dumbemployed.

AT WORK TODAY, I PACKED A BLUE TIE IN MY SUITCASE FOR A BUSINESS TRIP. I REALIZED AT THE HOTEL THAT I ONLY PACKED BLUE SHIRTS. I'M GOING TO LOOK LIKE A TESTING PATTERN. I'M DUMBEMPLOYED.

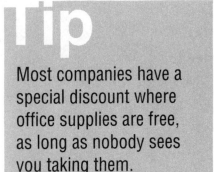

Most companies have a special discount where office supplies are free, as long as nobody sees you taking them.

At work today, I was tending bar for "cougar night." The attendees? Twenty twenty-five-year-old guys and exactly one cougar. Though I think she was more of a housecat. I'm dumbemployed.

At work today, our bar stopped holding out and purchased a TV. We used to be a classy place for intellectuals and poets. Now we host Monday Night Football. The worst part is that we make more money. I'm dumbemployed.

At work today, I returned from a two-week paternal leave. My desk was piled with trash. Apparently, the trashcan was too confusing for my cube mates. They didn't offer to clean. I'm dumbemployed.

Tip

If you've ever been sexually harassed by a coworker, you can probably get them fired by sleeping with someone in HR.

AT WORK TODAY, MY LABORATORY DECIDED TO ADD A REFRIGERATOR FOR BEER. WE THOUGHT IT WOULD BE A LOT OF FUN. THEN WE DISCOVERED THAT WE'D INCUBATED MOLD INCREDIBLY QUICKLY. THAT'S SCIENTIFICALLY DISGUSTING. I'M DUMBEMPLOYED.

At work today, I was head staffer at the coffee shop. I plugged my iPod into the stereo and played my band's music. I had two requests to "make it stop." I'm dumbemployed.

At work today, I saw a mommy and baby bird in their nest from my window. I was entranced by the scene—until the assistant manager told me to get rid of it. I'm dumbemployed.

At work today, I worked out during my lunch hour and showered at the gym. It took me twenty minutes in my cubicle to realize I was wearing my shower sandals. Even worse? I'd get in big trouble if anybody saw. I'm dumbemployed.

At work today, my coworker and I were both training to make a simple BLT. Apparently, I'm the only one who knew that T stood for "tomato," not "Tabasco." I'm dumbemployed.

AT WORK TODAY, I THOUGHT I WAS BEING A JUDICIOUS WORKER BY STAYING AT MY DESK INSTEAD OF HANGING OUT AROUND THE WATER COOLER. THEN I WAS CHIDED FOR NOT "INTERACTING" ENOUGH WITH THE "TEAM." YOU REALLY CAN'T WIN. I'M DUMBEMPLOYED.

At work today, I caught a draft blowing in. Unlike most drafts, this one was caused by an open front door. I have yet to successfully teach an employee, customer, or co-owner to close it. I'm dumbemployed.

At work today, I had to speak to someone from our company who is based in Australia. I'm in Iowa. It took me about twelve minutes to understand his name. I'm dumbemployed.

At work today, we were told that our company discount for Wii Fit is higher because "we need it." I'm dumbemployed.

Tip

If you need to gently tell a coworker about their bad breath, it's probably easier to just spray Binaca in their mouth when they're yawning.

At work today, I was reviewing quarterly numbers with a coworker when she suddenly started singing soul music. When I asked why, she told me that her therapist had told her to do it "when she was stressed." If you go around in public singing like that, you're going to be stressed a lot. I'm dumbemployed.

At work today, I had the honor of mowing a very large lawn. I'm sure that's exactly what my master's degree and three years in a PhD program prepared me for. I'm dumbemployed.

At work today, my coworker went on a twelve-minute tirade about being vegan. I know it was exactly that long, because she trapped me at the time clock before I could punch in. So it cost me time and money. I'm dumbemployed.

At work today, the printer was out of paper, but the office manager refused to get me more. Have you ever cut apart manila envelopes to use as printer paper? I have. I'm dumbemployed.

At work today, I put my coworker down as a reference for an apartment lease I'm signing. The landlord actually called me back and asked me if I was a drug dealer like my reference said. Remind me never to ask a practical joker for help. I'm dumbemployed.

Tip

Need a recommendation for your resumé? Just make sure to use your mother's maiden name instead of listing her as "Mommy."

AT WORK TODAY, A COWORKER DECIDED TO PLAY A GAME OF HIDE-AND-GO-SEEK WITH MY TIME CARD. HE SIGNALED IF I WAS CLOSE USING HOT AND COLD. I WAS COLD FOR ABOUT FORTY MINUTES. I'M DUMBEMPLOYED.

At work today, we were going to haze a new coworker who started working at our restaurant. While we were brainstorming, we realized we couldn't think of anything worse than the job itself. I'm dumbemployed.

AT WORK TODAY, I WAS ASKED TO TAKE THE COMPANY CAR TO THE GAS STATION TO FILL IT UP. I USED PREMIUM INSTEAD OF THE LOW GRADE. NOW THE DIFFERENCE IS COMING OUT OF MY PAYCHECK. I'M DUMBEMPLOYED.

At work today, I was sorting tomatoes when a child came up to me and asked for one. I handed it to her and she claimed that it was the funniest apple she'd ever seen. The mom didn't correct her. I'm dumbemployed.

At work today, I was capping a tooth for a patient who told me that he hated coming to the dentist. Just as I was putting on the cap, he kicked at me and nearly made me put the cap into his cheek. I'm dumbemployed.

Tip

Still haven't broken the ice with your cubicle mate? Start a staring contest without telling them.

At work today, they had me working with ties. A pleasant-looking middle-aged woman came up to me with two and asked me which one her husband would like better. I answer questions like that a lot, but usually the options aren't pink and hot pink. I'm dumbemployed.

COWORKERS' IDEAS

What if we pre-poured the ketchup on the fries? That way, we'd save money on bottles!

You know about our annual conference in Maui? Maybe we'd work harder in North Dakota.

What if instead of PowerPoint, we hand drew all our slides? It might be an inspiring project.

Instead of a Black Friday sale, why don't we raise prices? People will be curious why!

At work today, we realized why children aren't allowed in the store. Have you heard of a bull in a china shop? Try a five-year-old. It took me twenty minutes to clean up all the broken glass. I'm dumbemployed.

AT WORK TODAY, I SOLD A PAIR OF SCRUBS TO A GUY WHO COULDN'T HAVE BEEN MORE THAN FOURTEEN. HE WANTED PAJAMAS—WHICH IS WHAT AT LEAST A QUARTER OF OUR CUSTOMERS USE THEM FOR. I GUESS BEING A DOCTOR IS COMFORTABLE, ESPECIALLY WITHOUT THE PATIENTS. I'M DUMBEMPLOYED.

At work today, we had a company outing to the movie theater. Of course, company policy made it a lot of fun. To avoid lawsuits, we had to see a G-rated movie, even though our youngest employee is twenty-three. I'm dumbemployed.

At work today, I realized I hate cheeriness. My coworker Sheila responded to a possible downsizing at our firm by sending us all candy grams. Save your money, honey—you might need it. I'm dumbemployed.

At work today, an intern I supervise said that his necktie was really chafing him. He took it off and it turned out he'd left on the tag. He did it in case he wanted to return it. This is the caliber of intern I get. I'm dumbemployed.

At work today, it was time for a grandparents' special on cookies. A girl I work with said she wanted it because she had a grandchild. She's twenty-eight. You do the math. I'm dumbemployed.

At work today, we hired a specialist in viral marketing. She had a cold sore on her lip. I guess that's a good start. I'm dumbemployed.

AT WORK TODAY, I WAS SITTING AT MY DESK AND TALKING WITH ANOTHER COWORKER WHEN I SAID, "OH, THAT SUCKS." THE GUY I SHARE MY CUBE WITH THEN ASKED ME NOT TO USE EXPLETIVES IN THE WORKPLACE. I'M DUMBEMPLOYED.

At work today, I went through an airport security check with a coworker. He threw such a fit that we both got detained for suspicious behavior. I'm going to be branded a terrorist because of my coworker. I'm dumbemployed.

Tip

If you're working from home, you can play office politics by sucking up to your entertainment center.

At work today, I wore a thermal sweater since I was stuck in the garden section at our hardware store. No less than three people I work for asked me why I wore my underwear to work. I'm dumbemployed.

At work today, I had a broad mission to clean up the costume room. I didn't get very far. Is it so bad that I can't resist dressing up like a sixteenth-century wench? And that I had two people catch me doing it? I'm dumbemployed.

At work today, a competitor entered our store and started snooping around. My coworker told me to immediately give her a hard shove out the door. Such is the cutthroat world of stencil sales. I'm dumbemployed.

At work today, a teenager came in for a standard tune-up. His car was a BMW Z4. He didn't realize that he needed to change the oil more than once every two years. He drives that car and I'm in a Honda. I'm dumbemployed.

AT WORK TODAY, I WAS SUR-ROUNDED BY SPANISH SPEAK-ERS, WHICH IS TYPICAL AT OUR ARIZONA DINER. BUT HERE'S A TIP, GUYS: WHEN YOU LAUGH AND POINT AT ME, I HAVE AN IDEA THAT SOMETHING'S UP. I JUST HAVE TO SMILE AND TAKE IT, THOUGH. I'M DUMBEMPLOYED.

Tip

New coworkers have it hard enough already, so try to eliminate them as efficiently as possible.

At work today, the dog I was walking seemed listless. When the owner picked me up, she asked when I last fed him. I thought she had fed him. It turns out the dog hasn't been fed for two days. I'm dumbemployed.

At work today, I found that my entire office was wearing suits, except for me. They were all going to a special dinner. My job was to hold down the fort "just in case." I sat in silence for three hours. I'm dumbemployed.

At work today, I was working the front desk and was asked to hold a package for a tenant. I didn't realize they wanted me to literally hold it. A woman gave me her infant while she went for a jog. I'm dumbemployed.

IDEAS YOUR COWORKER SUGGESTS

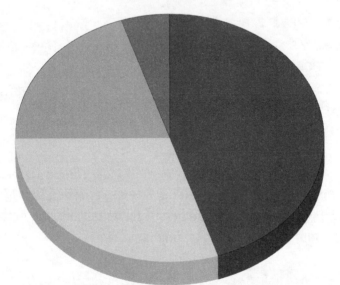

- WAYS TO HIT ON GIRLS
- PLANS FOR STEALING OFFICE SUPPLIES
- PRANKS ON YOUR BOSS
- THINGS RELATED TO WORK

At work today, we had a huge charity benefit in our banquet hall. I asked the attendees what charity the ball was helping. It took me three people to find one who knew. I'm dumbemployed.

At work today, I imposed a ban on my students against texting in class. I found out that one of them hollowed out his physics textbook just to fit a cell phone inside. I almost wanted to reward him. I'm dumbemployed.

AT WORK TODAY, I GAVE A HAIRCUT TO SOMEBODY WHO SAID HE WANTED A BUZZ CUT. WHEN HE WAS FINISHED, HE LOOKED DISAPPOINTED. "I'D JUST IMAGINED THERE'D STILL BE AN INCH LEFT." I'M DUMBEMPLOYED.

At work today, one of my coworkers talked politics with me for the first time. At first, I thought he was saying "Republicrats" as a joke about how the parties were the same—but I think he thought that was actually a party's name. I'm dumbemployed.

At work today, I hoped that we could forge a compromise on a crucial workplace situation. I was wrong—we're still filling a critical vending machine spot with Diet Cherry Dr. Pepper instead of Coke. I'm dumbemployed.

At work today, the girl I sit next to was crying. I asked her why, and she said it was because of her cat. I assumed it had died. Later, I found out that it had just been mean to her. It's a cat. I'm dumbemployed.

AT WORK TODAY, I HAD A GUY LOOKING FOR SUSPENDERS. WHEN I TOLD HIM WE DIDN'T HAVE THEM, HE WANTED ME TO GET HIM TWO BELTS TO USE TOGETHER. I'M DUMBEMPLOYED.

At work today, I shut the door to my office and, approximately thirty seconds later, was informed that I'm not actually allowed to do that. I'm dumbemployed.

Tip

Make your Friday especially casual by leaving your pants at home.

At work today, my parents were supposed to come in and visit me. They were late because my more charismatic coworker intercepted them and gave them my tour by himself. I'm dumbemployed.

At work today, the new employee asked for directions to the gym. Gym? Somebody got lied to in orientation. I sent him to the roof anyway. I'm dumbemployed.

AT WORK TODAY, WE INSTALLED A SCARECROW IN FRONT OF OUR GENERAL STORE. IT WAS A FAKE PROP TO LOOK FOLKSY. BUT IT STILL BOTHERS ME THAT PIGEONS PERCHED ON IT IMMEDIATELY. I'M DUMBEMPLOYED.

At work today, the sales guys took my fedora and tossed it back and forth for a while. Then they accidentally threw it out the window. I'm dumbemployed.

At work today, there was such a strong wind that my tie blew over my shoulder. I didn't notice until halfway through my meeting with the president of our company. I'm dumbemployed.

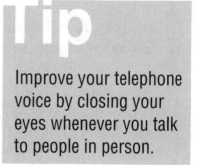

Improve your telephone voice by closing your eyes whenever you talk to people in person.

At work today, I stocked the reception area with magazines the doctor subscribes to: *People*, *Time*, and *Taxidermy Today*. I'm dumbemployed.

At work today, I swept leaves from our front walkway. It looked perfect, until government workers came by with leaf blowers and blew the leaves right back. I'm dumbemployed.

AT WORK TODAY, I GAVE A BRIEF LECTURE ON THE EARLY LIFE OF GEORGE WASHINGTON. THE COMMENT SHEETS I RECEIVED WERE INSIGHTFUL. MOST OF THE STUDENTS COMPLAINED THAT I DIDN'T MENTION THE CHERRY TREE. WHICH DOESN'T EXIST, OF COURSE. I'M DUMBEMPLOYED.

At work today, I showed up to work to find that my office had been split in half. Not only am I stuck sharing it, but I'm sharing it with an intern. He spent half the day telling me about his Ultimate Frisbee team. I'm dumbemployed.

At work today, I ate lunch in my car instead of in the company break room. My car frequently carries my dog and gets stuck in one-hundred-degree heat. But I think it smells better. I'm dumbemployed.

At work today, I parted my hair in a different direction because it's getting kind of long. Half the people in my office didn't recognize me. I'm dumbemployed.

At work today, I was the only person taking notes on a notepad instead of a laptop. I got mocked for being "analog." I was also the only one who wasn't surfing the Internet the whole time. I'm dumbemployed.

At work today, I went off script with a coworker and told him that I dislike my job. He nodded with me—and then told HR as soon as we finished talking. I'm dumbemployed.

At work today, there was an informal office poll about what we should serve at our holiday party. As usual, there was so much fighting about it that we were never able to make a decision. I'm dumbemployed.

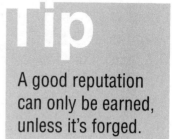

A good reputation can only be earned, unless it's forged.

At work today, the theme of the office became "holiday festive." The thing is, our decorator is a little overzealous. Really, who decorates this much for Flag Day? I'm dumbemployed.

At work today, I sold a gigantic jar of Muscle Milk to a football coach. I asked him what college his players attended. "They're in eighth grade," he said. I'm dumbemployed.

At work today, a union picketed outside our restaurant. After half an hour, they realized they had the wrong address. I'm dumbemployed.

Tip

Your company is like a family, if your family spent most of its time figuring out how to downsize you.

AT WORK TODAY, I WAS WORKING IN MY ARTIST'S STUDIO WHEN I HAD AN INTRUSION THROUGH MY WALL. BY WHICH I MEAN A HAMMER. MY LANDLORD DECIDED TO RENOVATE WITHOUT INFORMING ME. I'M LUCKY I GOT OUT ALIVE. I'M DUMBEMPLOYED.

At work today, they decided to name our kickball team Leaders of Sales, Eastern Region. Guess what the acronym for that is? I'm dumbemployed.

At work today, I was asked to rewrite our brochure to make us seem "less corporate." Of course, last time I checked, I work for a corporation. I'm dumbemployed.

At work today, my coworker suggested a great way to improve sales by 20 percent. I would have been happier if it weren't for the fact that I suggested it two weeks ago. I'm dumbemployed.

At work today, I was asked to find a new piece of property for a mini-mall. I've officially sold my soul. I'm dumbemployed.

At work today, I was fixing a toilet. I'm used to clogged toilets. Just not ones that are clogged with Wheat Thins. I'm dumbemployed.

At work today, my building began renovations. It's loud, dusty, and scheduled to last a minimum of sixteen months. I'm dumbemployed.

AT WORK TODAY, I DISCOVERED WRITING ON OUR BATHROOM WALL. IT WAS A PHONE NUMBER THAT TURNED OUT TO BE MY OFFICE LINE. THE REST IS TOO LEWD TO REPEAT. I'M DUMBEMPLOYED.

tip

Feeling guilty about taking a sick day? Inject yourself with a deadly virus in order to justify missing work.

At work today, I was really on a roll. I dropped three trays of plates and even managed to cut my ankle on one. I'm dumbemployed.

At work today, our little golf cart broke, so I ran boxes from our shed into the main room. I'm officially a mule. I'm dumbemployed.

IS YOUR COMPANY GOING OUT OF BUSINESS?

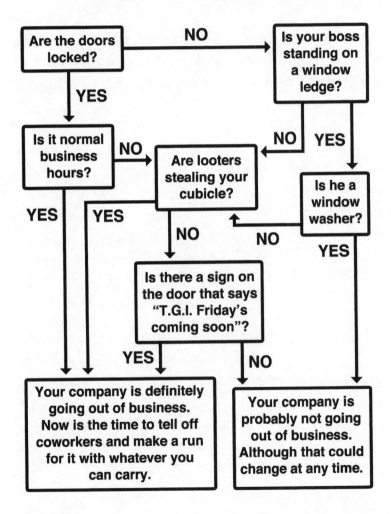

At work today, I looked up to notice that all of my business cards were gone. It turned out a coworker took a stack just in case he lost one of his. I'm dumbemployed.

At work today, I gave a brief presentation to a group of schoolchildren. Two of them left in the middle of my presentation because they were bored. I didn't think five-year-olds were allowed to do that. I'm dumbemployed.

At work today, my coworker proposed a "hypothetical scenario" in which he stole office supplies. I could see the stapler sticking out of his pocket. I'm dumbemployed.

At work today, we were supposed to start publicizing our new product. Naturally, we still haven't seen, touched, or used it yet. I'm dumbemployed.

AT WORK TODAY, I HAD A MORAL DEBATE WITH A COWORKER. APPARENTLY, HE THINKS THERE'S NOTHING WRONG WITH EATING AN UNLABELED SANDWICH FROM THE FRIDGE. THE SANDWICH WAS MINE. I'M DUMBEMPLOYED.

AT WORK TODAY, I TOOK IN A LITTER OF KITTENS DONATED TO OUR SHELTER. THE DONOR SAID SPAYING THE MOTHER WOULD HAVE BEEN CRUEL. I GUESS DROPPING OFF A BUNCH OF ORPHANS ISN'T? I'M DUMBEMPLOYED.

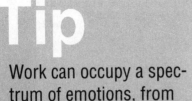

Tip

Work can occupy a spectrum of emotions, from "this is dumb" all the way to "this is stupid."

At work today, a shopper asked me where our mythology section was. I pointed him to it, but he came right back. Turns out he was actually looking for *Twilight* books. I'm dumbemployed.

At work today, our flight was delayed because a passenger forced me to explain the full responsibilities of the exit row before he decided it was too stressful. I'm dumbemployed.

At work today, I was replacing a printer cartridge. Why is it that empty printer cartridges always spill the most ink? I'm dumbemployed.

At work today, I served lunch to a pair having a business meeting. By the end, they were asking me for my opinion on leveraging the depleted housing market. But they could have really used help calculating my tip. I'm dumb-employed.

AT WORK TODAY, THE DUST AT WORK SETTLED AFTER A RECENT SHAKEUP. THOSE OF US WHO ARE LEFT SURVIVED DOWNSIZING. NOW, MANAGEMENT JUST THREATENS US WITH THE "STREAMLINING" TO COME. I'M DUMBEMPLOYED.

tip

One of the top reasons to become employed is for the unemployment checks when you're fired.

At work today, my desk chair broke, so I contacted the office manager. He said it would be a quick fix—only six to eight weeks. I'm dumbemployed.

At work today, we came across a Help Wanted ad for our workplace. The ad said "Literally anybody will be hired." I'm dumbemployed.

At work today, I heard my coworker humming and asked him to stop. I wish I hadn't. It at least kept him from belching. I'm dumbemployed.

AT WORK TODAY, WE LOST POWER HALFWAY THROUGH THE NIGHT. INSTEAD OF BEING PLUNGED INTO DARKNESS, I LIT CANDLES. LATER, I RECEIVED A PHONE CALL ON MY CELL THAT SOMEBODY HAD MADE A COMPLAINT ABOUT "SMOKING" IN THE BAR. I'M DUMBEMPLOYED.

At work today, I typed out invitations to the company party and realized that out of our 140-person company, I can recognize only ten people by face. I'm dumbemployed.

At work today, our staff went to happy hour together. Can I just say that, in certain cases, the "happy" part should be renamed? I'm dumbemployed.

At work today, eight new people all started work on the same day. And by the end of it, I saw at least two of them rereading their resumés and considering another job. I'm dumbemployed.

At work today, I signed for a package addressed to another employee. It was from Victoria's Secret. I'm dumbemployed.

At work today, I brought a McFlurry with me to my desk. My coworker asked if he could lick my spoon. I'm dumbemployed.

At work today, the guy who works the registers found a new way to vent his frustration. He hit me in my bad shoulder. I'm dumbemployed.

AT WORK TODAY, I USED MARKER ON OUR WHITE BOARD TO DRAW A CARICATURE OF OUR RECEPTIONIST. ONLY AFTERWARDS DID I REALIZE I HAD USED PERMANENT MARKER INSTEAD OF DRY ERASE. I'M DUMBEMPLOYED.

Tip

When buying things at your workplace, avoid confusing conflicts of interest by stealing them instead.

At work today, a coworker of mine blamed her late arrival on Daylight Savings Time, which ended an entire week ago. I'm dumbemployed.

At work today, I had a Jell-O mold hardening in our refrigerator for a work party. Apparently, some people took advantage of it. Now my Jell-O has a Post-it note inside, with "Freeze Faster" written on it. I'm dumbemployed.

At work today, I was asked to graph the correlation between our advertising spending and revenue. Is there a way to graph numbers lower than zero? I'm dumbemployed.

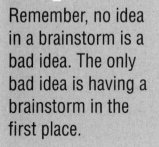

Remember, no idea in a brainstorm is a bad idea. The only bad idea is having a brainstorm in the first place.

At work today, I gave a tour of the famous tall building where I work. As my group rode the elevator up, one woman asked me if her brain was in danger from the pressure. I had an eight-year-old ask me that once. This woman was at least thirty-five. I'm dumbemployed.

At work today, I had to speak to a Japanese businessman. I tried learning one phrase in Japanese to talk to him. Afterwards, I found out that I asked him where the bathroom was. I'm dumbemployed.

WORK/LIFE BALANCE

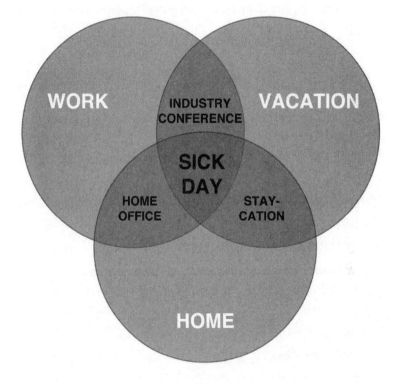

At work today, I was shelving things at my library and counting what I shelved. I realized I officially work more with DVDs than books. I'm dumbemployed.

At work today, I encountered my first counterfeit bill. It was hand drawn. I'm dumbemployed.

At work today, a guy set off our shoplifting detector. I had to pat him down—everywhere—to find the DVDs in his pants. I'm dumbemployed.

AT WORK TODAY, OUR PERPETUALLY BREAKING MICROWAVE BROKE AGAIN. MY LUNCH, WHICH WAS INSIDE, NOW INCORPORATES TINY PLASTIC SHARDS THAT FLAKED OFF THE INSIDE OF THE MICROWAVE. I'M DUMBEMPLOYED.

At work today, we gave a dog a long shampoo. That's typical. What isn't typical is that the owner requested we use conditioner she brought from home. I'm dumbemployed.

AT WORK TODAY, I OFFERED TO BEGIN AN OFFICE MARCH MADNESS POOL. ONLY ONE COWORKER KNEW WHAT MARCH MADNESS WAS. I'M DUMBEMPLOYED.

AT WORK TODAY, I FOUND OUT MY NEXT GIG INCLUDES ONE OF THE MOST FEARED WORDS IN THE ENGLISH LANGUAGE: UNITARD. I'M DUMBEMPLOYED.

At work today, I watched for two minutes as my coworker unstrung a string cheese stick. It was the most I've done today. I'm dumbemployed.

Tip

Your coworkers have great ideas, if you consider how smart they make you look in comparison.

At work today, I was having a terrible day and started ranting at the janitor. Only later did I realize he doesn't speak English. I'm dumbemployed.

At work today, my college wrote me about giving an alumni presentation. I thought it was an honor, until I learned the panel was titled "Changing Your Expectations." I'm dumbemployed.

At work today, my coworker actually gave me prank chewing gum. I'm thirty-eight-years-old and dealing with an emotional fifth-grader. I'm dumbemployed.

Tip

Office phones can't be put on vibrate, but you can shake your desk whenever you get a call.

AT WORK TODAY, I CONTINUED TEACHING MY CLASS HOW TO WRITE CURSIVE. ONE OF MY STUDENTS WROTE WITH A HIGHLIGHTER DURING HALF THE CLASS. I'M DUMBEMPLOYED.

At work today, one of my employees asked me to pay for their doggie daycare service because they were at work too long. I'm dumbemployed.

At work today, I was smoking a cigarette during my break when a young worker came out and asked to bum one. I asked him how old he was. "Fifteen," he said. "And a half." He was mad that I didn't give him one. I'm dumbemployed.

At work today, we rehearsed a portion of Handel's Messiah. In between each phrase of religious ecstasy, the conductor cursed at us. I'm dumbemployed.

At work today, I filled out state-required forms about our company's employees. We have three ex-convicts. That's almost half of our workforce. I'm dumbemployed.

At work today, I requested permission for learning a new program I need for my job. The supervisors wrote back that they'd just pay a consultant instead. And they wonder why they're over budget. I'm dumbemployed.

At work today, I asked for permission to bring in a chair, purchased with my own money. The office manager responded back that it would be "uncordial" for me to be more comfortable than anybody else. I'm dumbemployed.

AT WORK TODAY, WE UNROLLED OUR NEW SHIPMENT OF CUSTOM SOAPS. YUM. EXCEPT I'M CURIOUS IF THE BACON FLAVOR WAS REALLY A GOOD IDEA. I'M DUMB-EMPLOYED.

At work today, I was referring to a map of the United States when a coworker came up to me. "There we are," he said, pointing to Minnesota. We live in Wisconsin. I'm dumbemployed.

At work today, I was Googling a job applicant. Here's a tip, my friends. Don't put nude pics as your Facebook profile picture. 'Cause I'll see them. I'm dumbemployed.

At work today, some time passed and I was pretty bored. That's nothing unusual. I passed the time by popping virtual bubble wrap. Today, I got paid for busting 3,847 bubbles. I'm dumbemployed.

At work today, the subject of daycare came up. One of my coworkers asked me how I was handling being a single mom. I've been married for nine months. He's seen my wedding pics and has spoken with my husband. I'm dumbemployed.

Tip

An office holiday party is a great way to endanger your entire salary for a few free drinks.

At work today, I sent out emails telling our clients how much we value their business and that their work is "very unique." Only after I sent the emails did I discover that I'd pasted the entire list into the body of the email. I'm dumbemployed.

At work today, I pulled a muscle lifting some boxes from shipping to the store area. I asked for a back brace. I was given a roll of duct tape. "Just wrap it around real good," my supervisor said. I'm dumbemployed.

At work today, my coworker printed out a flyer asking for volunteers at the hospital. Unfortunately, he's not the best speller. I don't know how many responses we'll get, since we asked for "Candystrippers." I'm dumbemployed.

At work today, I told a potential customer about our storage units. She kept asking weird questions, like if it was heated and if it had a bathroom. Then she asked about the kitchen. "Ma'am," I said, "you know you can't live here, right?" She hung up. I'm dumbemployed.

AT WORK TODAY, I HELPED MY COWORKER MAKE A RESUMÉ FOR A NEW JOB. SHE SEEMED STUMPED BY THE "INTERESTS" SECTION. I ASKED HER WHAT SHE DIDN'T UNDERSTAND, AND SHE LOOKED UP AT ME WITH BIG SAUCER EYES. "WHY DO THEY WANT TO KNOW WHO I HAVE A CRUSH ON?" I DIDN'T BOTHER EXPLAINING. I'M DUMBEMPLOYED.

Tip

Struggling to get that raise you deserve? Help yourself! Your boss leaves the petty cash in the top right drawer.

At work today, I found out the "I" key on my keyboard doesn't work. So now every time I want to use it, I have to cut and paste. I'm dumbemployed.

AT WORK TODAY, I WAS ASSISTING A DOCTOR WITH SURGERY. THEY LISTEN TO MUSIC ALL THE TIME. BUT THIS TIME, THE CHOICE WAS PARTICULARLY INTERESTING. NEUROSURGERY AND 50 CENT. I'M DUMBEMPLOYED.

At work today, someone on our plane asked for the "Indian Kosher" meal. It was a blonde, twenty-year-old guy. I gave it to him and asked him if he was Hindu. "No," he said, "I just wanted to see what the hell Indian Kosher is." I'm dumbemployed.

At work today, I was trying to break in a new pair of jeans. I walked a little stiltedly. My coworker saw me and tapped me on the shoulder. "If you need to go to the bathroom, you can use that potted plant. I'll block you." I don't know why he didn't suggest the actual bathroom. I'm dumbemployed.

AT WORK TODAY, I WAS SUPPOSED TO GIVE A PRESENTATION ABOUT EMERGING MARKETS IN SOUTH AMERICA. I GAVE IT AND THOUGHT I DID OKAY. THEN I WAS ASKED WHY I DIDN'T TALK ABOUT EGYPT. UH, BECAUSE IT IS IN AFRICA, MAYBE? I'M DUMBEMPLOYED.

At work today, I developed photographs for a family. As you can guess, that's usually a barrel of laughs. Well, today's was terrifying. The whole roll was pictures of a hamster's funeral. Everyone was wearing black. I don't think that many people will come to my funeral. I'm dumbemployed.

tip

Be considerate of your coworkers' food allergies. Universally safe items include nuts and shellfish.

At work today, I helped a young couple plan their wedding. The guy rushed in late, but he was much more involved than the bride. I complimented him and he laughed. He was actually just her gay best friend. The groom was at home, watching baseball. I'm dumbemployed.

YOUR TURN!

At work today, _____

_____

_____

_____

_____

_____

_____

_____

_____I'm dumbemployed.

At work today, _____

_____

_____

_____

_____

_____

_____

_____I'm dumbemployed.

At work today, _____

_____

_____

_____

_____

_____

_____

_____

_____I'm dumbemployed.

At work today, _____

_____

_____

_____

_____

_____

_____

_____

_____I'm dumbemployed.

At work today, _____

_____

_____

_____

_____

_____

_____

_____

_____I'm dumbemployed.

At work today, _____

_____

_____

_____

_____

_____

_____

_____

_____I'm dumbemployed.

At work today, _____

_____

_____

_____

_____

_____

_____

_____

_____I'm dumbemployed.

At work today, _____

_____

_____

_____

_____

_____

_____

_____

_____I'm dumbemployed.

At work today, _____

_____

_____

_____

_____

_____

_____

_____

_____I'm dumbemployed.

At work today, _____

_____

_____

_____

_____

_____

_____

_____I'm dumbemployed.

OVERTIME

Who would expect that you'd work so hard for a job that doesn't even matter to you? Whether it's grubbing for a few extra hours' pay or scrambling for a meaningless change in title, we all work harder than we have to because we think it matters. By the time you figure out that overtime just means you work harder for less, it's too late. You've already signed up for another shift of ridiculousness.

At work today, I found thirty pallets of dog food in the back. When we made the order, somebody added a zero on the end. Now I have to either sell all the food or get rid of it. At this point, I'm considering chowing down. I'm dumbemployed.

At work today, I was asked to temp as a receptionist. Fine. I need the cash. But maybe it's not a good idea to have me at a veterinarian's office. I'm allergic to dogs, cats, and rabbits. I was sicker than all of the animals there. I'm dumbemployed.

At work today, I took my first sick day in two years. My boss told me it was fine—I'd be able to make it up by working on Saturday. I'm suddenly feeling sicker. I'm dumbemployed.

AT WORK TODAY, I HAD A SMOKE BREAK OUT BACK. IT LASTED THREE AND A HALF MINUTES, AFTER WHICH I WAS TOLD I NEEDED TO NOTE THE BREAK ON MY TIME CARD. I'M DUMBEMPLOYED.

At work today, I started my job as a chauffeur. Because I'm new, I got the "special cars." "Special" is code for smelly cars with stick shifts. I'm dumbemployed.

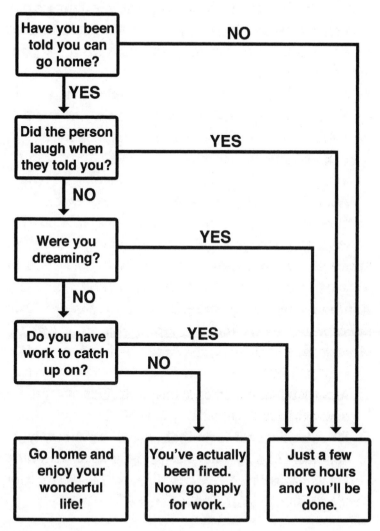

AT WORK TODAY, I HAD A GUY COME IN FOR A FISHING LICENSE. HE ASKED IF HE NEEDED A SEPARATE LICENSE TO USE EXPLOSIVES IN THE WATER. "IT'S STILL FISHING," HE SWORE. I'M DUMBEMPLOYED.

At work today, I was required to make phone calls. Predictably, I'm expected to use my own phone. I just donated three hours of talk time for telemarketing spam. I'm dumbemployed.

At work today, I was asked to research a three-year-old court case in Indonesia. Finding it wasn't hard. But translating it was. I'm dumbemployed.

At work today, my mother called while I was at work and talked to me for around thirty-five minutes. It was the most productive work I did all day. I'm dumbemployed.

At work today, the office manager decided she was sick of ordering pencils by herself. She made us fill out a request form that took at least twenty minutes. Glad my valuable time was used wisely. I'm dumbemployed.

At work today, I wore a collared shirt, tie, and suit jacket. I wouldn't mind if I didn't work as a waiter at a restaurant. Here's a tip: dress codes should only be required at places that pay more than $8 an hour. I'm dumbemployed.

AT WORK TODAY, I TRIED STREAMING MUSIC ON MY COMPUTER. THAT WAS THE BEGINNING OF A THREE-HOUR TOUR WHEN I LEARNED THAT MUSIC, VIDEO, AND NEWS ARE BLOCKED ON MY COMPANY COMPUTER. I HAVE TO, LIKE, WORK. I'M DUMBEMPLOYED.

At work today, the store was really over-crowded with tourists. How do I know? I was consistently asked directions to the street that we are on. And each time I had to answer with a smile. I'm dumbemployed.

At work today, I made a chunky granola mix that included raisins, nuts, chocolate, and dried fruit. I offered it to a customer at our coffee shop. "That's okay," he said. "I'll just have a candy bar instead." Three hours down the drain. I'm dumbemployed.

At work today, I carried about three pallets' worth of beer from my delivery truck into the store. Is it bad that every moment I work is like a taunt from God? I'm dumbemployed.

At work today, I discovered that I'm responsible for administering my company's Twitter page. It's official: even procrastinating has become work. I'm dumbemployed.

Tip

Bored on the clock? Time flies when you're having fun and/or methamphetamines.

At work today, I finally got the gumption to ask for a raise. I went into my boss's office to negotiate—and came out with a new project to do, three more assignments, and no extra money. Great negotiating, huh? I'm dumbemployed.

AT WORK TODAY, I WAS CALLED INTO THE ADMINISTRATIVE MANAGER'S OFFICE. SINCE I'M A LOWLY MAILROOM JOCKEY, I ASSUMED I MIGHT BE GETTING A PROMOTION. I DID, ALL RIGHT: I SPENT THE DAY COPYING HIS CD COLLECTION TO ITUNES. I'M DUMBEMPLOYED.

At work today, I installed my own space heater in my freezing cubicle. I was then informed that I can't use "company property." They meant the electrical outlet. It's going to be a long winter. I'm dumbemployed.

At work today, I skipped around in my work and did recreational stuff. I checked all my emails, updated my Facebook profile, and even looked up three ex-boyfriends. Time killed? Eight minutes. I work eight hours. I'm dumbemployed.

Tip

If you're scheduled to work a late shift, remember that a comfortable office chair can help. If that's not available, bring a hammock.

At work today, a project manager notified me that I'm going to be supervising three people. All three just graduated from college with degrees in English, art history, and political science. We're an engineering firm. It's going to be a long project. I'm dumbemployed.

AT WORK TODAY, I STAYED HALF AN HOUR LATE WAITING FOR AN EMAIL FROM A CLIENT. IT FINALLY ARRIVED: "TOO LATE NOW. I'LL EMAIL YOU TOMORROW." I'M DUMBEMPLOYED.

USING YOUR TALENTS IN THE WORKPLACE

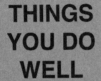

THINGS YOU DO WELL

THINGS YOU DO AT WORK

CHECK FACEBOOK

At work today, I gave three neck massages in a row to three weightlifter-type guys. I should really be paid extra to move muscles. I'm dumbemployed.

At work today, a guy ordered a drink called a Harvey Wallbanger. I offered a free gin and tonic instead, just so I wouldn't have to look it up. The guy made his own drink—and then didn't leave a tip. I'm dumbemployed.

At work today, I was supposed to plan a huge dinner for our company. I'm also organizing the tables. It's like a wedding between warring families—how do you seat people who hate each other? I'm dumbemployed.

At work today, I had a job interview. To get the interview, I had to submit a resumé, a report, and an "agenda." I found out that the next step involves another report. I don't even have a job yet, but I know one thing for certain: I'm dumbemployed.

At work today, one of the legs on my desk broke. I was told to make do. So now my company handbook is being used to prop up my desk. Fortunately, I know I won't need it. I'm dumbemployed.

Tip

If you feel like you're working too many hours, ask your boss if you can start measuring time in dog years.

At work today, I had to use a paring knife to carve out some fall pumpkins for the front of our doorway. It took me three hours to get the pumpkin right—after which the door knocked it into the path of a passerby who stepped on it. I'm dumbemployed.

At work today, I expected to have a decent day. I did, until about 4:30, which is when my boss finally told me to do something. I'm dumbemployed.

At work today, I found out that I have an allergic reaction to certain types of wool. I work in a clothing store in the sweaters section. I just hope that I get a discount on allergy medicine. I'm dumbemployed.

AT WORK TODAY, A PREGNANT WOMAN ENTERED OUR STATIONERY STORE. IN THE CARDS AISLE, SHE TURNED AND KNOCKED OVER A DISPLAY. HAVING A BABY IN YOUR STOMACH THROWS OFF YOUR BALANCE, I GUESS. AND GIVES ME MORE TO CLEAN UP. I'M DUMBEMPLOYED.

At work today, I had the honor of working in our basketball department. My job was pumping balls up. For eight hours. I'm dumbemployed.

At work today, I was trying to upgrade my work computer's iTunes, which I'm technically not supposed to do. Naturally, since I'm not supposed to do it, the process occupied my screen for at least half an hour. I was so afraid I'd get caught that I was trembling. I'm dumbemployed.

Tip

Overtime pay can help you buy all the happiness you've given up.

AT WORK TODAY, I WAS CALLED TO COMPRESS A DVD OF A COMPANY AWARDS CEREMONY ON MY OWN TIME. I THOUGHT IT WOULD TAKE FIVE MINUTES. IT TOOK FOUR HOURS. I HOPE PEOPLE REALLY LOVE RE-WATCHING JULIE'S PARODY OF *DANCING WITH THE STARS.* I'M DUMBEMPLOYED.

At work today, I had to type a memo about an assistant director in our company, whose name has five consonants and two vowels. Try spell-checking seventeen references to that. I almost fainted. I'm dumbemployed.

At work today, we installed a ceiling fan in our furniture store showroom. I spent the rest of the day cleaning up broken glass after the ceiling fan fell through our glass coffee table. I'm dumbemployed.

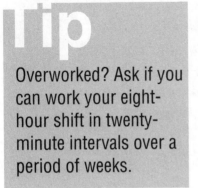

Tip

Overworked? Ask if you can work your eight-hour shift in twenty-minute intervals over a period of weeks.

At work today, I came out of the bathroom with wet hands because we were out of paper towels and I couldn't stain my nice work skirt. I wandered the hall for no less than four minutes searching for a carpeted cubicle wall. I'm dumbemployed.

AT WORK TODAY, I WAS SUPPOSED TO SHOW A COUPLE A HOUSE AT SEVEN P.M., WHILE IT WAS STILL LIGHT OUTSIDE. THEY SHOWED UP FOR IT AT NINE AND THEN SAID WE'D NEED TO SCHEDULE A SECOND VIEWING THE NEXT DAY TO SEE THE HOUSE IN NATURAL LIGHT. I'M DUMBEMPLOYED.

At work today, I got to listen to a twenty-minute speech about oil prices in China. All this was so I could try and sell a guy vinyl siding treatment. I wish I'd been in China. I'm dumbemployed.

At work today, I stayed late in order to catch up on some emails. As I shut down my computer, I heard a gasp. It was the janitor. When you scare the janitor, you know you've stayed too long. I'm dumbemployed.

Tip

Sometimes, it's best to have lunch at your desk. Make sure to unplug your hotplate when you're done cooking.

At work today, I was installing tiles on a roof with my brother. Here's a tip: don't leave your brother on the ground when you're on the roof. He pulled away the ladder and left me stranded for an hour. I'm dumbemployed.

At work today, I sold a cactus to a woman who was too shy to look me in the eye. She did manage to ask me if the plant would make her house warm like a desert. No, ma'am, the desert is not included. I'm dumbemployed.

At work today, I had on my suit. Then I found out that instead of giving a presentation on new national opportunities, I had to search through the supply room for a "vintage" corporate sign. My suit got all dusty. I'm dumbemployed.

At work today, one of my idiot coworkers decided to bring up politics. Since I lock up the building, I have to wait until everybody leaves. So because of a healthcare debate, I spent two hours waiting. I'm dumbemployed.

At work today, I started work at my hometown grocery after having to move back from the city. I answered the same question no less than three times: "What went wrong?" I'm dumbemployed.

At work today, the water cooler was empty, as it has been for three consecutive weeks. Instead, we are expected to get drinks from the bathroom tap. It tastes like rust-covered Styrofoam. I'm dumbemployed.

At work today, my boss asked me to send him a list of our products. I asked which products and he said all of them. We have over twenty-two thousand. I'm dumbemployed.

AT WORK TODAY, I WAS TOLD TO SKYPE WITH PEOPLE IN OUR SAN FRANCISCO OFFICE. IT TOOK US ABOUT A HALF HOUR TO ESTABLISH THAT THE WEBCAM SHOULDN'T BE POINTED AT OUR MARKETING DIRECTOR'S GUT. I'M DUMBEMPLOYED.

WHY WORK TAKES SO LONG

I really need some "me time." So we're gonna need you to work quadruple time.

You know that Word document you sent me? Can you write it by hand instead?

I saw that you cleaned the break room. Just so you know, that was also your break time.

You need to stay late to read the handbook. It's a great read—I wrote all 212 pages myself!

At work today, I thought I might be able to escape mopping duty by running out back and hiding against the wall. As I opened the door, I bumped into my boss. He put me on toilet work instead. I'm dumbemployed.

At work today, I gave a haircut to a guy with really long hair. That's fine. Except for the fact that he had a gallon of gel in it. I felt like I was chipping through ice. I'm dumbemployed.

AT WORK TODAY, WE HAD A FIVE-HUNDRED-PERSON TRACK MEET JUST DOWN THE ROAD FROM OUR VERY SMALL CONVENIENCE STATION. I DON'T KNOW WHY IT WAS HELD IN A TOWN AS SMALL AS OURS. BUT I DO KNOW THAT ONE OF THE BOYS TRIED TO BRING HIS JAVELIN IN WITH HIM. I'M DUMBEMPLOYED.

At work today, I cleaned the worst hotel room I've ever encountered. You know how annoying packing peanuts are to clean? I had to clean packing peanuts that had been shredded. I'm dumbemployed.

At work today, I was editing a company letter from a high-up mucky-muck to us peons. In the letter, he had some interesting quotes. One said: "Carelessness is next to Godliness." I'm dumbemployed.

At work today, I continued doing research for my professor, who is a renowned logician. That's why it's amazing that I had to spend ten minutes explaining to him why students would rather sleep in than show up for his 7:30 lecture. I'm dumbemployed.

Tip

Occasionally, you may have to stay late at work to finish all your Facebooking, Web browsing, and solitaire playing.

At work today, I had a bit of a raspy voice, which isn't great for a salesman. I had three clients apologize for making me talk to them. Now I sound like Gilbert Gottfried on a bad day. I'm dumbemployed.

At work today, I decided to try climbing up the corporate ladder. Instead, I spent six hours on a literal ladder, shelving textbooks ten feet in the air. My shoulders are sore from my ambition. I'm dumbemployed.

At work today, we needed some resistance to hold up a couple of boards. I've been in construction for thirteen years and am considered highly experienced. We used duct tape. I'm dumbemployed.

At work today, they had me drive from San Diego to LA to deliver a single folder full of documents. When I got back to San Diego, I found a voicemail telling me to be sure not to forget the second folder. I'm dumbemployed.

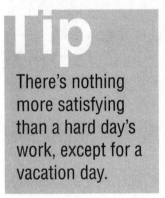

There's nothing more satisfying than a hard day's work, except for a vacation day.

At work today, I had to make about six smoothies at once. My manager surprised me with a $25 gift card. I thought it was a reward, but it was actually her way of thanking me for staying seven more hours until close. I'm dumb-employed.

At work today, I was appointed to supervise a group of seventh-graders playing Dungeons and Dragons in our store. They brought an entire case of Red Bull. I'm dumbemployed.

At work today, I requested three days off in the coming year. I was told that I could have two days off every week. Thanks, HR, but I'd actually heard of weekends before you told me about them. I'm dumbemployed.

At work today, my cubicle neighbor brought pictures of her kids to work after I teased her about not having any. I wish I hadn't made her bring them—I had to hear stories for over an hour. I'm dumbemployed.

At work today, the school buses lined up outside our school, but couldn't reach the drop-off station. Our principal had double-parked to make his commute easier. I had to corral two hundred kids while we waited. I'm dumbemployed.

At work today, I was refilling my water bottle when I discovered the water fountain was broken. Now, I have to travel up one stairwell and through three doors just to get a drink. I'm dumbemployed.

At work today, I was blissful in anticipation of Christmas break. My boss came into the room beaming. I thought he was happy for the same reason. But it was actually to announce our midnight day-after-Christmas sale. I'm dumbemployed.

At work today, my glasses were fogged and I wiped them on my shirt. My boss shouted at me to do it on my own time. I'm dumbemployed.

At work today, we all had to attend a speech being given by a high mucky-muck in the chemical-processing industry. Have you ever heard a three-minute joke about ethanol? I'm dumbemployed.

Tip

Caffeine can make your days go much faster, so make sure you know how to find a vein for direct injection.

At work today, I read an essay during my lunch break about productivity in the workplace. It said you should have a "friendly work environment" to work well together. I realized I hadn't talked to a single person all day. I'm dumbemployed.

At work today, I came into work for the first time with a leg cast. It took me ten minutes to travel from the front door to my cubicle, which I barely fit inside. Six weeks to go. I'm dumbemployed.

AT WORK TODAY, WE HAD A PORTRAITIST COME INTO OUR OFFICE TO TAKE PICTURES OF OUR LAWYERS. I HAD TO WAIT TILL THEY WERE FINISHED TO START MY WORK. IT TAKES A LONG TIME TO MAKE OUR STAFF LOOK GOOD. I'M DUMBEMPLOYED.

At work today, the credit card company called my work number to see if I wanted a new card. I talked for twenty minutes and am certain it was the most productive thing I did all day. I'm dumbemployed.

AT WORK TODAY, I DISCOVERED THAT THEY'RE MAKING OUR STORE SO COLD THAT WE HAVE TO WEAR A HAT AND GLOVES INSIDE. THEY TRY TO PRETEND IT'S FOR THE HOLIDAYS, BUT IT'S REALLY FOR SURVIVAL. I'M DUMBEMPLOYED.

At work today, I carried my entire team by working harder and longer than anybody else. My reward was a $5 coupon at the company gift store. I'm dumbemployed.

At work today, I had to clean out the gutters. We are conveniently located near a bank of trees and our building is incredibly high. The worst part, though, was that every customer decided to heckle me from below. I'm dumbemployed.

At work today, a guy I work with wanted to perform a magic trick to demonstrate some sort of sales principle. It took him four tries to succeed. I'm dumbemployed.

At work today, I wore a new pair of heels that broke five minutes into my shift. Since I didn't have any time to glue the heel back on, I enjoyed seven hours of limping. I'm dumbemployed.

At work today, I explained that as I put my key into my bike lock, the key had snapped off. I got assigned a night shift as punishment for my tardiness. I'm dumbemployed.

At work today, my coworker tried reverse psychology on me and it worked. He said that I didn't have discipline in the restaurant. Now I'm working weekends through next month. I wish I'd taken a psych class in high school. I'm dumbemployed.

At work today, I stepped on my glasses ten minutes into my shift. Have you ever tried waiting on tables that you can't even see? I said "sir" to a lot of women. I'm dumbemployed.

AT WORK TODAY, THEY HAD US WRITE DOWN OUR JOB RESPONSIBILITIES. I NEEDED MORE THAN ONE PAGE TO DO IT. MY SALARY IS DEFINITELY ONE-PAGE CALIBER, THOUGH. I'M DUMBEMPLOYED.

WHY YOU'RE WORKING LATE TODAY

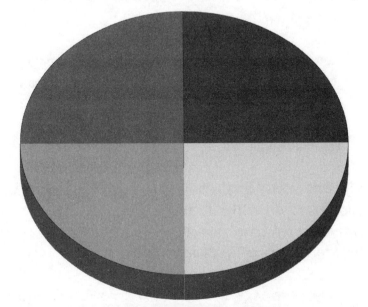

- ■ COWORKER "SICK"
- ■ BOSS FORGOT TO DO IT
- ■ DOING 7 PEOPLE'S WORK
- ■ GUNNING FOR 1.2% RAISE

At work today, they blocked Facebook, Twitter, and NYTimes.com on the corporate Internet. But they still haven't figured out a way to block Spider Solitaire. I'm dumbemployed.

At work today, I lost my balance as I was stacking a large supply of ketchup containers. They fell on the floor, which would have been fine if I hadn't fallen on them. I look like I'm bleeding to death now. I'm dumbemployed.

At work today, I left early to vote, which I'm legally allowed to do without any punishment. But apparently my boss didn't get the memo. I got extra overtime for fulfilling my civic duty. I'm dumbemployed.

AT WORK TODAY, I MADE A LITTLE OBSERVATION THAT THE OFFICE WAS DIRTY. THREE HOURS LATER, WE WERE STILL CLEANING IT BECAUSE OF MY COMMENT. I'M DUMBEMPLOYED.

At work today, I tried scanning a picture into our copier. It's supposed to be advanced and easy to use. Fifteen minutes later, I only had copies of my hand. I'm dumbemployed.

At work today, I had to call customers for a survey about customer satisfaction. It turns out that our scale didn't go low enough for our customers. I'm dumbemployed.

At work today, my boss thought it would be funny to give us all lumps of coal for our Christmas bonus. It would be funny, if an actual bonus followed it. None did. I'm dumbemployed.

Tip

Conserve printer ink by printing only things that are white.

At work today, there was an all-company alert that computer hackers are targeting our network. I would be scared. But I know for a fact that our most sensitive corporate data is pictures of various people's cats. I'm dumbemployed.

AT WORK TODAY, I DISCOVERED A THICK GEL COVERING THE SURFACE OF OUR KITCHEN'S COUNTER. APPARENTLY, SOMEBODY DECIDED TO EXPERIMENT WITH CORN SYRUP. I GOT TO CLEAN IT UP. I'M DUMBEMPLOYED.

At work today, I decided to push for a real corporate handbook. Instead, I got a printout of the Ten Commandments and was told to revise it. I'm dumbemployed.

Tip

Too much to do? Most assignments are flammable.

At work today, I packed for our office move. I never knew you could get cardboard calluses. I'm dumbemployed.

At work today, we were asked to search for a lost child in our furniture store. After two hours, we found him hiding in a dining room cabinet. He never explained why he hid there. I'm dumbemployed.

At work today, we discovered that our building is being foreclosed. Our office provides financial consultation—just not to the right people, apparently. I'm dumbemployed.

AT WORK TODAY, THERE WAS AN INTENSE DEBATE ABOUT WHAT COLORS WE SHOULD USE FOR OUR FOLDER TABS. THE DEBATE LASTED NO LESS THAN FORTY MINUTES AND ENDED UNRESOLVED. I'M DUMBEMPLOYED.

At work today, I was asked to work with an artist on our new logo. He wants to do something abstract. We sell vinyl siding. I'm dumbemployed.

At work today, I went about storing hamburger patties. We freeze them all, of course. So I spent four hours traveling into a freezer and out, carrying fake meat. I'm dumbemployed.

If you're working long hours, double-check your watch.

At work today, I gave violin lessons to a six-year-old prodigy. She is a Suzuki violinist, however, so I got to hear her shout at me that my classical training was wrong. I'm dumbemployed.

AT WORK TODAY, A BRIDE CAME IN FOR A FITTING. SHE ASKED FOR SOMETHING LOW-CUT THAT SHOWED A LOT OF LEG. BUT NOT "TOO SLUTTY." CONTRADICTION MUCH? I'M DUMBEMPLOYED.

At work today, I had to apply for thirteen different permits so that we could plant a tree in front of our building. I'm dumbemployed.

Tip

Balance your work life and home life using a very large scale.

At work today, something felt familiar about one of our clients. The reason? He calls in the same order for a single shirt every week. Apparently, buying more than one is not on his agenda, but making me do the paperwork is. I'm dumbemployed.

At work today, a woman came to our bank and said her house was underwater. I told her mortgage default is normal. She told me that she'd literally been flooded. I have a lot of paperwork to do. I'm dumbemployed.

AT WORK TODAY, I WAS DESIGNING A NEW CASE FOR A BOARD GAME WE PUBLISH. ONLY WHEN I WAS FINISHED DID I LOOK AT THE BOARD GAME AND REALIZE I'D DRAWN THE WRONG ONE. I'M DUMBEMPLOYED.

At work today, I found a cartoon taped to the microwave depicting an angry little man who looks a lot like me. Now I'll spend the entire workday traipsing around the office trying to figure out who hates me. I'm dumbemployed.

At work today, I got a taste of my own medicine when a coworker called in sick and left me working. The difference is that he claims to have mono. I'm looking at six weeks covering his shifts. I'm dumbemployed.

At work today, I submitted a third revision of a letter my boss had me write. His comment was that I needed to make it smarter, like him. I'm dumbemployed.

At work today, we hired a DJ to play during our art gallery's show. I had to spend a half hour explaining to him why gangster rap wasn't appropriate. I'm dumbemployed.

AT WORK TODAY, I ACCEPTED DEFEAT AND TOOK MY CO-WORKER'S SHIFT. HIS STATED REASON WAS THAT HE HAD A FUNERAL. BUT I SAW HIM BUYING PREEMPTIVE HANGOVER MEDICATION ON THE WAY OUT. FUN FUNERAL, I GUESS. I'M DUMBEMPLOYED.

Tip

You can save energy at work by taking power naps from nine a.m. to three p.m. every day.

AT WORK TODAY, WE MADE AN ELABORATE DESIGN FROM CANNED SWEET POTATOES. THAT'S WHEN A FIVE-YEAR-OLD BARRELED INTO THE STORE AND DECIDED TO MAKE A FUNNY. NOT ONLY DID THE DESIGN CRASH, BUT THE KID GOT INJURED TOO. I'M DUMBEMPLOYED.

At work today, I ate my lunch in my car just to avoid my coworkers. By the time it was over, I had a mild case of sunstroke, which was still preferable to a mild conversation. I'm dumbemployed.

At work today, I discovered that our employee handbook contradicts itself. It says we shouldn't be overworked. Then it gives us time and a half for overtime. Guess which one I'll follow. I'm dumbemployed.

Tip

Outshine your coworkers by having office chair imprints on your body.

At work today, I closed two accounts with our firm. One of them moved to another firm and the other went bankrupt. I spend more time when I'm closing an account than when I open one. I do it more often, too. I'm dumbemployed.

WORKING GRAVEYARD SHIFT

- If you can't stay awake, remember that public nudity usually provides an adrenaline rush.

- Feeling lonely? Report a robbery attempt. The police will be happy to keep you company until they find out you lied.

- If you've always wanted to be on a reality show, you can pretend the security cameras are filming you.

- Drinking coffee is overrated, especially when you can inject it directly into your veins.

- It's daytime somewhere. Find company by making calls to Australia on the company phone.

- Since you're all alone, nobody will know if you leave for half of your shift and go home.

At work today, they wanted me to order more paper supplies for the office. Then they told me I needed to negotiate a 60 percent discount, which I'm pretty sure doesn't exist unless the paper is made of cardboard. I'm dumbemployed.

At work today, a seventeen-year-old kid told me I was past my prime. Thing is, when it comes to being a movie usher, he's probably right. I'm dumbemployed.

AT WORK TODAY, I WAS SEALING ENVELOPES WITHOUT ANY GLUE OR SPONGE. MY TONGUE HAS MORE PAPER CUTS THAN MY FINGERS. I'M DUMBEMPLOYED.

At work today, I took out the trash, as usual. Except that last night's banquet was the biggest in our history. Have you ever taken out fifty bags of trash? I'm dumbemployed.

AT WORK TODAY, ALL OUR TABLES WERE FULL AND I WAS TOLD TO SEAT PEOPLE AT THE BAR. WHEN THE BAR WAS FULL, I WAS TOLD TO SEAT PEOPLE OUT-SIDE. WHEN THAT WAS FULL, I WAS TOLD TO SERVE PEOPLE STANDING UP AND HAVE THEM HOLD THEIR PLATES. I'M DUMBEMPLOYED.

At work today, I discovered that all of my lab rats had died overnight. They didn't die because of anything I injected—they died because the heating pipes exploded. I'm dumbemployed.

At work today, I silenced my phone during a conversation with a coworker and forgot to switch it back. When I finally checked my phone, I found that someone had called me eight times. I'm dumbemployed.

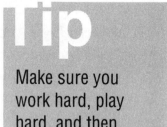

Make sure you work hard, play hard, and then blame other people hard.

AT WORK TODAY, I BROUGHT HEADPHONES IN ONLY TO FIND OUT, ABOUT FIFTEEN MINUTES LATER, THAT THEY ARE BANNED IN THE EMPLOYEE HANDBOOK. I'M DUMBEMPLOYED.

At work today, I was collecting train tickets and saw a thirteen-year-old guy try to evade me. I spent my entire shift chasing him for a $3.15 fare. I'm dumbemployed.

At work today, there was a small chemical spill in our lab. I mopped it up and a coworker came in, shocked. "You should wear a mask or you could die." Well, by then it was too late. I'm dumbemployed.

At work today, I spent my entire shift converting text files to Microsoft Word. Have you ever added spaces by hand on a three-hundred-page document? I'm dumbemployed.

Tip

An expectant mother may claim to be going into "labor." Remind her that without a time card it isn't real work.

AT WORK TODAY, THEY HAD US FILING AWAY ALL OF OUR CONTRACTS FROM THE TWENTIETH CENTURY. THAT'S FINE. WHAT WASN'T FINE WAS THAT THEY APPARENTLY DIDN'T USE FOLDERS BACK THEN. I'M DUMBEMPLOYED.

At work today, I gave physical therapy to twenty adolescent boys. I'm a middle-aged woman. Let's just say that they were very excited to get leg massages. Too excited. I'm dumbemployed.

At work today, I flew from Denver to Dallas. I now have people at the Denver McDonald's that recognize my face because I'm there so often. I'm dumbemployed.

AT WORK TODAY, THERE WAS A LOVELY COPPER CLASP ON THE SUITCASE I USED TO CARRY AN IMPORTANT SET OF CONTRACTS AND BROCHURES. SO LOVELY THAT IT SNAPPED RIGHT OFF WHILE I WAS IN THE MIDDLE OF A CROSSWALK. I SINGLE-HANDEDLY STOPPED MANHATTAN TRAFFIC. I'M DUMBEMPLOYED.

At work today, I had to put up the new movies on our sign outside. We have to use individual letters to do it, and I ran out of T's. I spent my day trying to arrange lowercase l's to be legible as T's. I'm dumbemployed.

At work today, they replaced my great work cell phone with an inferior one that cost $5 less. Now everything takes twice as long. I'm dumbemployed.

At work today, one of my fellow cops returned from a two-week suspension. You'd think he'd be eager to work. Instead, he asked me for a magazine to take into the bathroom. I'm dumbemployed.

AT WORK TODAY, WE WERE AT THE NEGOTIATING TABLE FOR OVER THREE HOURS. THE AMOUNT IN DISPUTE? $58.44. I'M DUMBEMPLOYED.

Tip

By working on major holidays, you earn the right to note on your resumé that your soul has been destroyed.

At work today, I was assigned to help my coworker's daughter learn our filing system. After eight hours, I'm still not convinced she's literate. I'm dumbemployed.

At work today, we launched our new website. It says everything about us—except for how to contact us to actually buy something. Now I have to fix it. I'm dumbemployed.

At work today, I asked if I could have off for my sister's wedding. The scheduler asked me if she could have it on another day instead. I'm dumbemployed.

At work today, I was asked to correct grammar on a company document. Unfortunately, the document comes from outsourced Indian writers. Someone should tell them that "educationment" isn't a word. I'm dumbemployed.

At work today, I started debugging code written by the previous team. The first note on the code was left by a previous programmer. It said "I'm sorry." I'm dumbemployed.

At work today, I got yelled at for being a jerk. The same coworker later asked me to cover for him that night, and for some reason I did it. I'm dumbemployed.

At work today, I was asked to compromise on my demands from my employer. They wanted me to take less money and work more. I asked what the compromise was, and they said that I was being allowed to stay. I'm dumbemployed.

tip

You can make time pass more quickly by speeding up the clocks.

AT WORK TODAY, I REALIZED THAT I HAVE CALLUSES, NOT FROM MANUAL LABOR, BUT FROM THE AMOUNT OF TIME I'VE HELD A SPATULA. I'M DUMBEMPLOYED.

At work today, they asked me if I really needed a bathroom break. My employers actually forgot I'm a human being and not a robot. I'm dumbemployed.

At work today, I subbed for a friend who is having a baby. Then I did my own shift. That means I've been inside a Denny's for fifteen hours straight. I'm dumbemployed.

At work today, I found a single rose on my desk. I thought it was a romantic gift at first, but it turned out to be an initiative produced by HR. I'm dumbemployed.

At work today, there were about three hundred pieces of mail that came in. For some reason, they used only initials on the letters, so I had to look up every employee name and match them up. Did I mention it was only junk mail? I'm dumbemployed.

At work today, I was called up to the front of the store and put on lost-and-found duty. All day, all I do is page the entire building and see if anybody lost a hat, a coat, or a child. I'm dumbemployed.

AT WORK TODAY, THEY ANNOUNCED THAT OUR VACATION DAYS WERE BEING RESTRUCTURED. TRANSLATION: I NOW HAVE THREE FEWER DAYS EACH YEAR TO ESCAPE TO ASPEN. I'M DUMBEMPLOYED.

At work today, I was emailed four different online petitions from my coworkers. I spend more time dealing with spam than doing real work. I'm dumbemployed.

At work today, I was yelled at by my boss for "leaving early" at 6:00. My shift ends at 5:30. I'm dumbemployed.

AT WORK TODAY, WE THOUGHT THAT BRINGING ON SOME EXTRA TEMPS MIGHT MAKE WORK A LITTLE EASIER. WE SPENT TWO EXTRA HOURS OF WORK TRAINING THEM. THEN THEY QUIT. I'M DUMBEMPLOYED.

At work today, I got a really late call to help open a door for somebody who was locked out of her car. I didn't want to go, but a job's a job. When I got there, the lady was crying. Her problem was pretty sad, too—she'd been turning the key in the wrong direction. I'm dumbemployed.

At work today, my boss held a special meeting. Apparently, he's been reading some business guru's book. The guy will be in San Diego later this month. My boss says we all have to go hear him speak. The worst part? We're paying for the tickets ourselves. I'm dumbemployed.

At work today, I got to update my restaurant's "Fan Page" on Facebook. I think the owner thought it was his personal account—so far, he's posted some Screamo, quotes from the Bible, and pictures of himself. Shirtless. I have a lot of work to do. I'm dumbemployed.

Tip

If you say you need a day off because your grandmother died, it's fair that you ask Grandma to take one for the team.

AT WORK TODAY, I WAS PUTTING AWAY BOOKS, WHICH I USUALLY DO ONCE A WEEK. THIS WEEK, HOWEVER, I WAS ASSIGNED TO THE BUSIEST SECTION, WHERE PEOPLE ARE ALWAYS READING AND MOVING BOOKS: EROTICA. I'M DUMBEMPLOYED.

At work today, I needed to download some software for a project I am working on. The network staff refused because it would use the company's Internet bandwidth. Of course, it costs them more to keep me idle for the rest of the day until I can go home and download it there. I'm dumbemployed.

At work today, I showed up five minutes early. I always do that. Then I realized: five minutes over 250 days a year is 1,250 minutes. I work twenty extra hours a year. I'm dumbemployed.

AT WORK TODAY, I STAPLED TOGETHER PACKETS ABOUT OUR FRANCHISE. EACH PACKET WAS NINETY-EIGHT PAGES LONG. HAVE YOU EVER TRIED TO STAPLE SOMETHING THAT SIZE? I THINK I BROKE SOMETHING IN THE PROCESS. I'M DUMBEMPLOYED.

At work today, they had us working outdoor security for an arts event. Apparently, this year they wanted to make it easier for the artists. That means they can leave all of their crappy paintings and sculptures overnight. And I have to work the overnight shift to guard them. I'm dumbemployed.

At work today, our IT department began a terrible new policy where we have to submit all the websites that we want to visit on our work computers. That's the reason I stayed an hour late today trying to figure out why YouTube was necessary for work. I'm dumbemployed.

At work today, we were classifying all the people in our office. The hot girl. The smelly guy. The weird old dude. We ended up classifying 220 people by the end. No overlap. What a day. I'm dumbemployed.

Tip

If you want to work less overtime, consider joining a carpenter's union. It may help if you're a carpenter, too.

At work today, I got promoted to a position as a supervisor with more responsibility. I was hoping for a raise. Instead, I still get paid the same amount as when I started working there two and a half years ago. I'm dumbemployed.

YOUR TURN!

At work today, _____

_____

_____

_____

_____

_____

_____

_____

_____I'm dumbemployed.

At work today, _____

_____

_____

_____

_____

_____

_____

_____I'm dumbemployed.

At work today, _____

_____

_____

_____

_____

_____

_____

_____

_____I'm dumbemployed.

At work today, _____

_____

_____

_____

_____

_____

_____

_____I'm dumbemployed.

At work today, _____

_____

_____

_____

_____

_____

_____

_____

_____I'm dumbemployed.

At work today, _____

_____

_____

_____

_____

_____

_____

_____I'm dumbemployed.

At work today, _____

_____

_____

_____

_____

_____

_____

_____

_____I'm dumbemployed.

At work today, _____

_____

_____

_____

_____

_____

_____

_____

_____I'm dumbemployed.

At work today, _____

_____

_____

_____

_____

_____

_____

_____

_____I'm dumbemployed.

At work today, _____

_____

_____

_____

_____

_____

_____

_____I'm dumbemployed.

WEIRD SHIFT

It's incredible that every day of work manages to be so undeniably weird. Coworkers, customers, bosses, and everybody else have demands that boggle the mind and leave an unpleasant taste in your mouth. If you've ever wandered through an abandoned attic, you know what work can feel like on the weirdest days. The strangest part of all is that we pretend it's normal.

At work today, I practiced my "serious salesman voice." I performed it for one of my coworkers. He frowned and touched my shoulder. "You sound like Foghorn Leghorn after a stroke." So that's why my sales are so bad. I'm dumbemployed.

At work today, I received a call from the IRS. They want to audit me because they think my reported income is suspiciously low. Nope, guys. That's actually what I get paid. I'm dumbemployed.

At work today, I noticed a car alarm going off in our parking lot, so I paged everyone in the store. Then the alarm stopped. I assumed the customer had turned it off. Later, I assisted in filing the police report for the stolen car. Whoops. I'm dumbemployed.

Tip

A full freezer uses less energy. Buy frozen taquitos in bulk and do your part to save the environment.

AT WORK TODAY, MY ASSISTANT SAID SHE HAD SOME GOOD NEWS: SHE HAD RECEIVED A PROMOTION. NOW, TECHNICALLY AT LEAST, MY ASSISTANT IS MY BOSS. JUST AN AVERAGE MONDAY. I'M DUMBEMPLOYED.

AT WORK TODAY, I HAD A COWORKER ASK ME WHAT TYPE OF SHAMPOO I USED. I TOLD HIM. "IT SMELLS GREAT," HE SAID. THE PROBLEM IS THAT I HAVE NO IDEA WHEN HE WAS SMELLING MY HAIR. I'M DUMBEMPLOYED.

At work today, I cried after a particularly bad shift waitressing. My manager came over to me. I thought it was to ask me what was wrong, but he actually just wanted to make sure I hadn't leaked onto the food. I'm dumbemployed.

At work today, I gave computer classes to my very old coworker. I spent the first ten minutes explaining that "blog" wasn't a dirty word. I'm dumbemployed.

At work today, I cleaned out the keyboard keys on my computer. I've never eaten lunch at my desk— so why did I find so much rice? I'm dumbemployed.

At work today, my son called me from his school. At first, I was worried something was wrong. But he just asked me if I was having another miserable day. You know things are bad when your kid starts asking you that question. I'm dumbemployed.

AT WORK TODAY, I FOUND A POST-IT NOTE TAPED TO MY COMPUTER SCREEN ASKING ME TO TURN DOWN MY RADIO. I WAS MAD FOR FIVE MINUTES BEFORE I REALIZED THAT I DON'T HAVE A RADIO. I'M DUMBEMPLOYED.

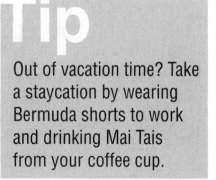

Out of vacation time? Take a staycation by wearing Bermuda shorts to work and drinking Mai Tais from your coffee cup.

At work today, I went to a convention in my industry. They had about one hundred nametags made up for us—and exactly zero Sharpies. I squinted at ballpoint pen scrawls all day. I'm dumbemployed.

At work today, my office announced a cost-cutting measure. Guess who's writing office memos with golf pencils? I'm dumbemployed.

AT WORK TODAY, I WAS GIVEN A LECTURE ABOUT THE FINGERNAIL POLISH I WORE NOT BEING "PROFESSIONAL" ENOUGH. MY COLOR? SHIMMER NUDE. APPARENTLY, "NUDE" WOULD BE MORE RESPECTABLE. I'M DUMBEMPLOYED.

BAD EXCUSES FOR CALLING OUT

I'm being robbed right now, so I can't make it in at the moment.

Can't come in tonight. The president needs my help. He says I'm the country's top waiter.

Hey boss, I need the day off. My baby is sick. Also, I have a baby now.

I can't make it in today. The snow is too hard to navigate, especially in my roller skates.

At work today, I didn't finish work until around 5:30. As I left, I set off three motion sensors. I guess my office becomes a haunted house ten minutes after close. I'm dumbemployed.

At work today, I burped in front of my coworker. At first, I was embarrassed. Then he said, "Exsqueeze me." At least I wasn't embarrassed anymore—for myself. I'm dumbemployed.

At work today, I took a cell phone picture of a company event and emailed it to my boss. Except that I emailed him the wrong one. I really shouldn't keep pictures from "slutty Halloween '09" on my phone. I'm dumbemployed.

AT WORK TODAY, A CHILD AND HIS MOTHER CAME INTO OUR DAYCARE. I WAS INFORMED THAT THE CHILD IS "ALLERGIC" TO COLD. UH, HOW IS HE ALIVE? WE LIVE IN MINNESOTA. I'M DUMBEMPLOYED.

At work today, I emailed with a coworker to decide on our lunch date. It took us thirteen emails to come to a decision. First, that's way too many. Second, we are only fifteen feet apart. I can understand why this company is screwed. I'm dumbemployed.

AT WORK TODAY, I WANTED TO HAVE A BRIEF DISCUSSION WITH HR ABOUT MY HEALTHCARE BENEFITS. AFTER TWENTY MINUTES OF CONSULTING, WE REALIZED THAT NEITHER OF US UNDERSTOOD IT. GREAT SIGN! I'M DUMBEMPLOYED.

Tip

Working with friends can make a job more fun. There's room for at least two people underneath your desk.

At work today, I put sugar in my coffee for the first time and discovered, after pouring, that it was salt. My office is a playground for pranks that nobody even notices. Somehow, that's sadder. I'm dumbemployed.

At work today, I was asked to cut company spending, which my coworker described as an "impossible problem." Here's a tip: an $88-cheese plate might not be a necessity. I'm dumbemployed.

At work today, I played a tape of *Sesame Street* in daycare. I thought that would be a safe bet. I was wrong. Apparently, the parents complained that Snuffleupagus is too phallic. I'm dumbemployed.

At work today, I logged into Facebook and saw that my coworker had sent me a friend request. That wouldn't be unusual, except that it's the third time I've had to ignore a request from him. I'm dumbemployed.

At work today, the elevator was moving really slowly, so I asked the janitor what was going on. "Oh, it'll break down any day now." Now my blood pressure rises each time I have to go to the ground floor. I'm dumbemployed.

AT WORK TODAY, MY COWORKER ASKED ME IF I THOUGHT DOLPHINS WERE REALLY SMARTER THAN PEOPLE. "SMARTER THAN PEOPLE?" I ASKED. "OR YOU SPECIFICALLY?" BECAUSE A HALIBUT IS SMARTER THAN HE IS. I'M DUMBEMPLOYED.

At work today, I had turkey for lunch and one of my coworkers complained about second-hand tryptophan drowsiness. That's not how it works. I'm dumbemployed.

At work today, I left my iPod on my desk when I went to the bathroom. When I came back, my coworker was listening to it. "Possession is nine tenths of the law," he said. I'm dumbemployed.

Tip

In a global economy, you'll be annoyed by people all around the world.

At work today, I received a gift certificate from HR as a "reward for friendliness." It wasn't a real gift certificate, though, just a 20 percent off coupon for Office Depot. I think they might have just found it in the mail. I'm dumbemployed.

AT WORK TODAY, MY COWORKER WOULDN'T SPEAK UP. I KEPT ASKING HIM TO TALK LOUDER, AND HE EVENTUALLY PASSED ME A POST-IT NOTE. "I'M CONSERVING MY VOICE," IT READ, "FOR REALLY IMPORTANT CONVERSATIONS." I'M DUMBEMPLOYED.

At work today, I received a thank-you note intended for the doctor I work for. The note thanked him for "curing all the diseases." I may be wrong, but I'm pretty sure the doctor isn't explaining things fully to a few people. I'm dumbemployed.

At work today, I brought my MacBook Pro to work and got called, in front of everyone, "a sissy." I didn't even know that word still existed. I'm dumbemployed.

AT WORK TODAY, I WAS REPORTING ON A CITY COUN-
CIL MEETING AND REALIZED THAT I'D BEEN TO MORE
OF THE MEETINGS THAN THE CITY COUNCIL MEMBERS.
I'M DUMBEMPLOYED.

At work today, forty-year-old moms were having a "mall walk marathon." I was stationed right at the turning point all day and felt like I was going to be smothered by middle-aged women. I'm dumbemployed.

At work today, I was doing stand-up com-
edy in the strangest place I've ever performed. Do people really come to a diner to
see stand-up? I'm dumbemployed.

At work today, my phone didn't get any reception at
all during the entire day. That was bad since I use it
as my GPS. I wandered the highway all day without
finding a single meeting place I was supposed to go
to. Is it bad that I enjoyed it? I'm dumbemployed.

At work today, I was required to wear a tie, but realized at the last minute that I didn't know how to
put it on. I had to have the female secretary tie it
for me. I'm dumbemployed.

At work today, I was reviewing the expense report that my employees submitted. Call me crazy, but something tells me that $114 spent at a restaurant called Miss Charlene's Teasers is not legitimate. I'm dumbemployed.

tip

As technology becomes more important in the workplace, you may be required to speak in a robot voice.

At work today, I listened to my radio. I always use my headphones and crank up the volume. At about 3:15, I turned around to see that three people were making bunny ears behind me. I'm dumbemployed.

At work today, one guy in our office came in wearing a Batman costume. Cool! But Halloween was a week ago. Now I'm afraid. I'm dumbemployed.

AT WORK TODAY, I DID WHAT I LIKE TO CALL MY BIG SALE VICTORY DANCE. EVERYBODY IN THE DEPARTMENT DOES IT—BUT NOT EVERYBODY HAS THE MANAGER START GRINDING UP BEHIND THEM. I'M DUMBEMPLOYED.

At work today, my coworker came to work wearing flip-flops. That would be fine if we weren't auto mechanics. I'm dumbemployed.

AT WORK TODAY, A GUY WITH AN MMA T-SHIRT CAME INTO THE RESTAURANT AND SAT DOWN. HE ATE THREE OMELETS, TWO PLATES OF BACON, AND THREE PANCAKE PLATES. I ASKED IF HE WAS IN TRAINING. "I'M NOT A FIGHTER," HE SAID. "I'M JUST HUNGRY." I'M DUMBEMPLOYED.

At work today, our company got a fresh shipment of bubble wrap for mailing. Is it bad that we probably popped more of it for fun than we'll ever use? I'm dumbemployed.

At work today, my business cards came in. According to the typo, I'm director of HR, which stands for "Human Regulations." So I'm either God or a dictator now. I'm dumbemployed.

At work today, I decorated a cake with a superhero design. But the message was "Happy Birthday, Grandma." Something doesn't fit. I'm dumbemployed.

Tips for Your First Day at Work

DO

Get a company business card

Tackle new work

Enjoy a break in the lunchroom

Look like a professional

DON'T

Get a company tattoo

Tackle new coworkers

Break the lunchroom

Look like a professional wrestler

AT WORK TODAY, I WAS TRANSLATING A SPANISH CUS-
TOMER'S ORDER TO THE PHARMACIST. THEY WANTED THE
PHARMACIST TO GIVE THEM CLARITIN, SUDAFED, AND BREAD.
I HAD SOME EXPLAINING TO DO. I'M DUMBEMPLOYED.

At work today, I received a sneer from a diner, so
I asked why. She answered like it was obvious.
"You forgot to put ketchup on my steak." I'm dumb-
employed.

*At work today, I was day-trading stocks when a coworker
interrupted me to talk about some cooking show. When I
finally broke away, I turned to my computer. A discussion about tomatoes cost me $1,100. I'm dumbemployed.*

At work today, I catered a black tie event.
Usually, you can depend on those to be
pretty classy. This time, I encountered a
black tie that had clearly been made out of
a dress sock. I'm dumbemployed.

At work today, there was a guy outside my building with a
cardboard sign. Instead of saying "The End of the World
Is Near," it said "Quit Your Jobs to Live." I officially agree
with a crazy person. I'm dumbemployed.

At work today, my coworker performed his Arnold Schwarzenegger impression. He's the only person in the world who thinks Arnold is British. And he still makes more money than I do. I'm dumbemployed.

At work today, I forgot to bring my toothbrush. Why do I need a toothbrush, you ask? Because every day, my coworker forces me to taste his beef jerky. Today's vintage was called Jalapeño Death Squad. I'm dumbemployed.

At work today, some of my campers complained that there was a monster in their bunk. I assumed they were being idiots and ran inside. A bat flew right into my chest. I'm dumbemployed.

Tip

As Thomas Edison once said, genius is 1 percent inspiration, 99 percent perspiration, and 10 percent math.

At work today, I got in touch with a wholesaler about buying a time clock. He then asked me if I was eighteen or older. Are there really seventeen-year-olds trying to buy these? And is it illegal? I'm dumbemployed.

At work today, a labeled Tupperware container in the break room fridge said, in all caps, "DO NOT EAT. HIGHLY VALUABLE." I got a little excited thinking it might be something cool. Inside it? Dry broccoli. I'm dumbemployed.

At work today, I taught a trainee about automation in the canning process. After it was over, he asked me if the robots were going to turn on us. He wasn't joking. I'm dumbemployed.

AT WORK TODAY, MY SHIFT CONCLUDED AND I WENT TO MY LOCKER, PUNCHED OUT, AND LEFT THE BUILDING AT EXACTLY 11:11. I MADE A WISH. IT DIDN'T COME TRUE, THOUGH—I STILL HAVE TO WORK TOMORROW. I'M DUMBEMPLOYED.

At work today, we served a dish with a "bold" and "chunky" taste. I guess that means someone spilled too much pepper into some rotting cabbage. I still had to claim it was delicious. I'm dumb-employed.

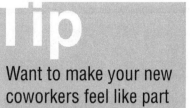

Want to make your new coworkers feel like part of the team? Try an ice-breaker like spin the bottle or freeze tag.

AT WORK TODAY, I FOUND A HIDDEN CACHE OF CANDY IN A SUPPLY CLOSET. I LOOKED AT THE DATE ON THE BAGS, AND IT WAS FROM FOUR YEARS AGO. THEN I REALIZED THAT'S THE CANDY THAT GOES IN OUR CANDY DISH UP FRONT. I'M DUMB-EMPLOYED.

At work today, I was scrubbing down a chair when I found a new piece of graffiti on a table. It said "Ted Loves Ted." Was Ted his boyfriend? Or did he just have great self-esteem? I'm dumbemployed.

At work today, I double-checked sources for my dissertation. It turns out that a major portion of my thesis is based on a scholar who was discredited for making up half of his conclusions. I don't know which half I'm using. I'm dumbemployed.

Tip

Safety at the workplace is important—always wear a bulletproof vest.

At work today, we sold the last Christmas tree of the season. Today's date is January 2. All I have to ask is who buys a Christmas tree in January? Especially a nine-foot one. I'm dumbemployed.

At work today, I guided a tour group through our vine-yard. One of the tourists asked me where the "wine tree" was. I'm dumbemployed.

At work today, we received a tip from a client for a party. There are four of us, but the supervisor just took the whole tip because he thought he worked the hardest. I'm dumbemployed.

AT WORK TODAY, A YOUNG WOMAN CAME INTO THE DEPARTMENT STORE AND ASKED WHERE THE DRESSING ROOM WAS. SHE DIDN'T BRING ANY CLOTHES—SHE JUST DISAPPEARED INSIDE. I'M DUMBEMPLOYED.

tip

Looking to make some spare cash? Remove and sell all recyclables from the office trash bin.

At work today, I had a guy from the coffee shop follow me to my bus stop. I thought he was going to ask me out. Instead, he asked me if my male coworker was single. And gay. I was actually offended. I'm dumbemployed.

At work today, I took my laptop to a coffee shop. When I went to the bathroom, I left it on my seat. It's gone now—including the thirty-page document I was working on. I'm dumbemployed.

AT WORK TODAY, I LOCKED MY BIKE TO A PARKING METER. ONE OF THE GENIUSES I WORK WITH ASKED ME WHY I DIDN'T FEED THE METER WHEN I WALKED AWAY. I'M DUMBEMPLOYED.

At work today, I was on Craigslist looking for an apartment. That's when I saw a listing for a job like mine, with $10,000 more for the salary. I'm dumbemployed.

Tip

A great job includes benefits, like healthcare, daycare, vacation days, and, occasionally, a salary.

At work today, I showed a couple a dream home in a really nice suburb. They were happy with it, except for the fact that the house didn't come with a lawn mower. Guys, that's not how houses work. I'm dumbemployed.

SEARCHING FOR WORK

work from home	✕	Search

About 162,500 results (0.21 seconds)   Advanced search

▶ **Did you mean: *unemployment checks***

jobs for english majors	✕	Search

About 42,300 results (0.13 seconds)   Advanced search

▶ **Did you mean: *jobs for waiters***

gifts for your boss	✕	Search

About 23,700 results (0.16 seconds)   Advanced search

▶ **Did you mean: *regifting for your boss***

bonding with your coworkers	✕	Search

About 88,200 results (0.11 seconds)   Advanced search

▶ **Did you mean: *hiding from your coworkers***

At work today, my office fantasy football league concluded and I realized it's the only reason that I went in to work. I'm dumbemployed.

AT WORK TODAY, I FILLED UP A "HAPPY BIRTHDAY" BALLOON FOR A WOMAN AND ASKED HER WHEN THE BIG DAY WAS. "NEXT MONTH," SHE SAID. "BUT I WANTED TO GET THE BALLOON EARLY JUST IN CASE." I'M DUMBEMPLOYED.

At work today, we put up a sign in our office that said "No. 1 Regional Distributor of Flax Seed Products in the State." Is there a No. 2? I'm dumbemployed.

At work today, I had to get a signature for a package that was addressed to a dog. A human signed. A paw print wouldn't have fit on my reader. I'm dumbemployed.

At work today, my mother asked me exactly what I do in my financial services job. I told her, after which she asked me why I couldn't have an easy-to-understand job like my brother. He works at a drive-thru. I'm dumbemployed.

At work today, the omission of $30 from my paycheck caught me off guard. It turns out it was intentional— I'd gotten a cut without being notified. I'm dumbemployed.

At work today, there was a delivery customer who wanted us to bring two bottles of Pepsi with his order. I told him we only had Coke. He canceled the order immediately. I'm dumbemployed.

AT WORK TODAY, I PUT A FEW MINUTES OF TIME INTO PLANNING OUR COMPANY PARTY. MY COWORKER SAID THAT EGGNOG WAS ESSENTIAL, WHICH WOULD MAKE SENSE IF IT WEREN'T JULY. I'M DUMBEMPLOYED.

At work today, a co-worker pulled me aside to perform some impressions. I expected George W. Bush or Jack Nicholson. Instead, all of them were people in his family that I had never met. I'm dumbemployed.

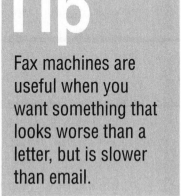

tip

Fax machines are useful when you want something that looks worse than a letter, but is slower than email.

At work today, I tried to convince a coworker to take a shift for me. Instead, I convinced him to quit. I'm dumbemployed.

tip

Did you know that Russian workers carry most of their discussions around the vodka cooler?

AT WORK TODAY, MY CHAIR WAS DIAGNOSED WITH BEDBUGS. I WASN'T SURPRISED. I'M DUMB-EMPLOYED.

At work today, a couple sent back their salmon for being too fishy. Is it bad that theirs was the best meal I've eaten all week? I'm dumbemployed.

At work today, I did an electrical job for a small house. First tip: don't plug four extension cords into one outlet. I'm dumbemployed.

At work today, my coworker said that I showed incredible determination. I asked him why, and he said that the fact I hadn't quit yet was incredible. I'm dumbemployed.

At work today, I brought in a plate to hide in the cupboard at work. This is what I've stooped to just to retain a little dining dignity. I'm dumbemployed.

At work today, my lunch of carrots earned me the nickname of "Bugs" around the office. And by today, I mean three years ago. It's lasted that long. I'm dumbemployed.

At work today, we were forced to gut one of the hotel rooms. In the process, we found three Barbie dolls embedded in a wall. I guess ghosts like to play, too. I'm dumbemployed.

At work today, some painters covered our office with a final coat. I didn't know that, of course, which is why I leaned against the wall to tie my shoe. I'm dumbemployed.

AT WORK TODAY, I GOT BOOKED FOR A VIOLATION OF COMPANY POLICY. MY TRANSGRESSION WAS THAT I WORE BLACK JEANS INSTEAD OF BLUE JEANS. I'M DUMBEMPLOYED.

Tip

When you're fired, it never hurts to make a good impression on your boss's face.

At work today, I decided to check if there was some justification for the fact that we get only one fifteen-minute break during an eight-hour shift. There is: my boss hasn't read the labor laws. I'm dumbemployed.

At work today, I met the guy that I'll be working with on a new advertising campaign. His name is Suave. I'm dumbemployed.

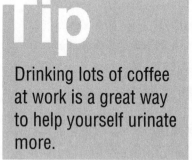

Drinking lots of coffee at work is a great way to help yourself urinate more.

AT WORK TODAY, DAYCARE TAUGHT ME QUITE A FEW LESSONS. MAX HELPED ME LEARN ABOUT BIOLOGY. IT TURNS OUT THAT GREEN SNOT ISN'T JUST A MYTH. IT WAS PRACTICALLY NEON. I'M DUMBEMPLOYED.

At work today, I was asked to modify a '70s suit lapel. I assumed they wanted to take it in. They actually wanted the opposite. That decade's never even existed. I'm dumbemployed.

At work today, I judged a drawing contest our store sponsored. It wasn't hard since there were only three entries. I'm dumbemployed.

At work today, we were given new uniforms to reflect our company's modern redesign. It looks like our owner thinks that sequins are modern. I'm dumbemployed.

At work today, my monitor started emitting smoke. The IT guy told me to wait until it starts smelling. I'm dumbemployed.

At work today, I got my invitation to the company party. It might be the only one in the world that's BYOB. I'm dumbemployed.

At work today, I was really thirsty and drank from the water fountain on the floor. My manager said it was for customers only. I feel like I'm in a civil rights movie. I'm dumbemployed.

AT WORK TODAY, I ISSUED A CHALLENGE TO MYSELF: NO COFFEE, ALL DAY. I LASTED FORTY-TWO MINUTES. I'M DUMBEMPLOYED.

At work today, I sold some guitar picks to a cute girl, so I asked her how long she'd been playing. "All my life," she said. "I love the piano." I'm dumbemployed.

Tip

Job candidates should be evaluated on their education, experience, and dimples, in reverse order.

AT WORK TODAY, I WAS SELLING MOVIE TICKETS TO A PERSON. HE BOUGHT THREE FOR HIMSELF, SO THAT HE'D BE SURE TO HAVE A BUFFER SEAT ON BOTH SIDES. I'M DUMBEMPLOYED.

Tip

Corporate retreats are great for bonding, but try to avoid nudist ones.

At work today, I was looking at my coworker's notepad during our meeting. On the top in big letters it said "DON'T LOOK AT MY NOTEPAD AGAIN." I'm dumbemployed.

AT WORK TODAY, I DISCOVERED MY BUSINESS'S PHILOSOPHY OF GOOD CUSTOMER SERVICE: HIDE. I'M DUMBEMPLOYED.

At work today, there was a lake of ketchup on the floor of our restaurant. I asked the staff why nobody had cleaned it up. Apparently, they were all worried it might be blood. I'm dumbemployed.

At work today, a politician asked if he could put fliers on our counter. I said that it was reserved for merchandise. He then shouted that he'd "show me" when he became president. I'm dumbemployed.

At work today, my girlfriend came to my workplace to see me. But before she could, my coworker insisted on "helping" her with her purchase. She had to pretend she was buying something and then actually buy it. I'm dumbemployed.

At work today, my boss revealed that he'd lost all of our time sheets for the month, but he says he'll handle it by using his imagination. I don't like the way he thinks. I'm dumbemployed.

Tip

Blogging can be a great way to advance your career, as long as your career is cat-watching.

At work today, my coworker learned about IM. I received thirty messages in the span of a minute. Most of them were "Am I doing it right?" I'm dumbemployed.

AT WORK TODAY, I PRICED REDUCTIONS ON OUR PRODUCE. IT TURNS OUT THE ROTTEN FOOD IS ONLY ABOUT 10 PERCENT LESS THAN THE RIPE STUFF, ACCORDING TO OUR FORMULA. I'M DUMBEMPLOYED.

WHAT'S THAT WEIRD SMELL AT WORK?

At work today, I timed how long I could work without interruption. Over the course of eight hours, my highest time was ten minutes and thirty-eight seconds. I'm dumbemployed.

At work today, I decided to raid our work refrigerator. All I found was hummus, a mini bottle of rum, and a jar of jelly. Is it bad that I was satisfied with that? I'm dumbemployed.

AT WORK TODAY, THE CABLE GUY WAS DIGGING BEHIND OUR BAR AND FOUND AN OLD SIGN. IT WAS NEON AND STILL WORKED WHEN WE PLUGGED IT IN. THE ONLY PROBLEM IS THAT IT WAS A SIGN FOR OUR BIGGEST COMPETITOR. I'M DUMBEMPLOYED.

At work today, I respectfully declined to participate in the company potato sack race. My lack of spirit seems to be rare. Turns out that even Helen, our wheelchair-bound employee, participated. I'm dumbemployed.

At work today, they had us do a fire drill. The fire inspector seemed to enjoy giving a particularly graphic description of our "charred bones" if we didn't listen to him. I didn't catch the rest of what he said. I'm dumbemployed.

AT WORK TODAY, I THOUGHT I SAW A CELEBRITY ENTER OUR JEWELRY STORE. INSTEAD, IT TURNED OUT TO BE AN ASPIRING SHOPLIFTER. I'M DUMBEMPLOYED.

At work today, my students came back from a two-week vacation. Apparently, it was a working vacation for them, however: they learned curse words. I'm dumbemployed.

At work today, we discussed limiting coffee breaks. Now we're getting three minutes instead of five to slurp up a cup. I'm dumbemployed.

At work today, a Communist distributed flyers in our coffee shop. She did it shortly before buying a $5 latte, which is more than I can afford. I'm dumbemployed.

At work today, I gave tennis lessons to a typical middle-aged mom-type. She asked me to help her with her backhand—and then I felt a pat on the bottom when I was finished. I'm dumbemployed.

AT WORK TODAY, I SWAM BEFORE WORK. THE PROBLEM? I WORK AS A CHEF. MY STEAK TARTARE TASTED LIKE CHLORINE THE ENTIRE DAY. I'M DUMBEMPLOYED.

At work today, I got to learn about my coworker's new cat. That would be tolerable, if it weren't the fifth one I've heard about. I'm dumbemployed.

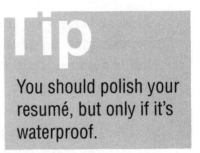

You should polish your resumé, but only if it's waterproof.

At work today, we got a new soundboard in our daycare. It cost more than I make in a couple of months. I'm dumbemployed.

AT WORK TODAY, WE RECEIVED THE NEW PAINT FOR OUR SPE-CIAL KIDS' CENTER IN OUR GYM. THE COLOR THEY ORDERED? DARK BROWN. I'M DUMBEMPLOYED.

At work today, I was at work when I got a sub-poena. The allegation? Charging somebody incor-rectly in the checkout line. I threw it away, so I really hope it was a joke. I'm dumbemployed.

At work today, I went to Starbucks to pick up an order for my entire office. I came back into the cu-bicle with eight full cups of coffee when my coworker stopped me and frowned. "Oh," she said, "We wanted tea." I'm dumbemployed.

At work today, I spent almost twenty minutes trying to log into my computer, but my password just would not work. Only at the end did I realize that I had Caps Lock on. I'm dumbemployed.

Tip

If you're concerned about outsourcing, move to India and try to get your old job.

AT WORK TODAY, I BROUGHT MY GUITAR IN TO WORK AND HID IT IN THE BREAK ROOM. BY BREAK TIME, ONE PERSON WAS ALREADY PANTOMIMING SMASHING IT OVER THE TABLE. I'M DUMBEMPLOYED.

At work today, I gave a cave tour to a group of first-graders. At least three of them told me they wanted to be vampires when they grew up, which is why they wanted to meet bats. I'm dumbemployed.

At work today, we had an after-work party. Jan from marketing shouted that we should play some party music. She put on smooth jazz. These are the wild people I work with. I'm dumbemployed.

At work today, I sold a lovely heirloom necklace to a very young woman. Later on, I saw it wrapped around her ankle like a bracelet. I'm dumbemployed.

At work today, there were about thirty boxes of shirts from Brazil in our warehouse. I found a tarantula in the first one I opened. I'm dumbemployed.

Tip

Though you should give out your business cards, try not to throw them at people.

AT WORK TODAY, I ENGAGED A COWORKER IN A TOTALLY REASONABLE DISCUSSION. UNFORTUNATELY, IT WAS ABOUT TV. AS SOON AS WE SWITCHED TO WORK, YELLING WAS INVOLVED. I'M DUMBEMPLOYED.

At work today, I slogged away on a spreadsheet and realized I was making tiny explosion noises each time I put a figure in. I'm dumbemployed.

At work today, we installed a rug in our front hallway to stop people from slipping. Nobody thought to put anything under the carpet, though. Two people have already fallen. I'm dumbemployed.

At work today, I gave physical education tests to the kids in my class. I had at least ten kids who couldn't do a single pull-up. I'm dumbemployed.

At work today, I was playing online poker when I got a tap on my shoulder. It was the IT guy. I thought I was in trouble. But he was just desperate to watch something fun happen. I'm dumbemployed.

Tip

Want a promotion? Just pick the office you want and camp out there until you get the job.

At work today, they had me writing a new slogan for our company, but it got rejected for being "too grammatical." I'm dumbemployed.

At work today, terrorism came to our mailroom. Our company was sent a package full of dog crap. I opened it. I'm dumbemployed.

AT WORK TODAY, I BEGAN WORKING IN MY FATHER'S OFFICE. SOMETHING TELLS ME I'M THE ONLY EMPLOYEE WHO WAS THREATENED WITH A SPANKING. I'M DUMBEMPLOYED.

WORK IN THE FUTURE

- In order to increase efficiency, cubicles will be replaced by pyramidicles.

- Bureaucracy will disappear in favor of robotocracy, where several different robot executives reverse each other's decisions.

- All business transactions will involve an elaborate chain of call centers calling call centers. Eventually, you will ask yourself for assistance.

- Workers will save time by teleporting to work; unfortunately, the security check will take about an hour and a half.

- Coffee breaks will change to refueling breaks.

- Minimum wage will soar to $10.25.

At work today, two southern women ordered grits. I am a waiter at an Indian restaurant, so our grits selection is lacking. They didn't understand. I'm dumbemployed.

At work today, my computer screen developed a huge crack right down the middle. My boss suggested that I tape over it. I'm dumbemployed.

AT WORK TODAY, WE INSTALLED A NEW BULLETIN BOARD IN THE BREAK ROOM. IT MUST HAVE TAKEN LESS THAN TEN MINUTES FOR IT TO FILL UP WITH PICTURES OF MY COWORKER RORY'S CATS. I'M DUMBEMPLOYED.

At work today, our IT guy accidentally blocked every website instead of just YouTube and Facebook. The result? Productivity increased at least 30 percent. I'm dumbemployed.

At work today, we were ordering food supplies for the next week. Whoever did it apparently decided that potatoes weren't necessary even though we serve fries with every meal. I'm dumbemployed.

At work today, they had us run a waxer on the grocery floor. Have you ever crashed into a five-foot-tall display of tomato cans? Because I have. I'm dumbemployed.

At work today, I learned that I've been left out of an email convo intended for me. The reason? They had been emailing "Stew." My name is Michael. How do you get those two mixed up? I'm dumbemployed.

At work today, the equestrian wing of our company made an unexpected appearance. That means that my boss's daughter insisted on bringing her horse inside the department store. The household-goods section doesn't smell so good anymore. I'm dumbemployed.

Tip

When cleaning your workplace, remember that many of your coworkers could use a scrubdown as well.

At work today, we realized that moss wasn't going to grow on most of the rocks near our national park. Our solution to the problem? All day today, I had a green paint can in my left hand and a brush in my right. I'm painting moss on rocks. I'm dumbemployed.

At work today, my work uniform shrunk in the laundry. I now look like I'm a stripper parodying my job. Trust me—I don't have a stripper's body. I'm dumbemployed.

At work today, I had a shifty-eyed guy come in and ask to have keys cut. He wanted about thirty copies of the exact same key. "I'm having a party," he blurted out. I didn't ask what kind of party it was. I'm dumbemployed.

Tip

Though it's true there's no business like show business, there's also no business like plumbing!

At work today, I asked one of my interns to collate some fliers. "Yes, sir!" he said, and literally saluted. Fifteen minutes later, he came back. "And what exactly does 'collate' mean, sir?" I'm dumbemployed.

AT WORK TODAY, I CALLED MY GIRLFRIEND AND HEARD A GUY'S VOICE IN THE BACKGROUND. MY GIRLFRIEND SAID IT WAS NOTHING. A FEW MINUTES LATER, MY COWORKER CAME IN SWEATY. AND HE SMELLED LIKE HER PERFUME. THANKS, SWEETIE. I'M DUMBEMPLOYED.

At work today, I began to reconsider my choice of employment. I install cable. The house I just installed cable at was falling apart at the walls. I saw a dead roach on the floor and a young kid in a homemade diaper. They got HBO, of course. I'm dumbemployed.

At work today, we shredded a bunch of bills that came into the office. Only afterwards did I learn they hadn't been paid yet. I'm dumbemployed.

AT WORK TODAY, I WAS AT THE PHOTO COUNTER IN OUR DRUGSTORE. A CUSTOMER CAME IN WITH A ROLL AND SAID THE PHOTOS WERE "TOP SECRET," SO I LOOKED, OF COURSE. THEY WERE JUST FAMILY PICTURES. WAS IT A SECRET FAMILY, OR SOMETHING? I'M DUMBEMPLOYED.

At work today, we had a pimply fourteen-year-old boy come in saying he wanted to use our tanning machines. I asked him why. "It's warm. It's private. And they clean it up when you're done." I'm dumbemployed.

At work today, I realized that my favorite website was blocked. The reason? "Lewd content inappropriate for work." The website? Google.com. I'm dumbemployed.

At work today, I found a strange cylinder next to the time clock. I opened it and found a pile of white pills inside. My boss saw it, too, and popped a pill. "Worth a try," he said. I did the same. I'm dumbemployed.

YOUR TURN!

At work today, _____

_____

_____

_____

_____

_____

_____

_____I'm dumbemployed.

At work today, _____

_____

_____

_____

_____

_____

_____I'm dumbemployed.

At work today, _____

_____

_____

_____

_____

_____

_____

_____

_____I'm dumbemployed.

At work today, _____

_____

_____

_____

_____

_____

_____

_____

_____I'm dumbemployed.

At work today, _____

_____

_____

_____

_____

_____

_____

_____

_____I'm dumbemployed.

At work today, _____

_____

_____

_____

_____

_____

_____

_____

_____I'm dumbemployed.

At work today, _____

_____

_____

_____

_____

_____

_____

_____

_____I'm dumbemployed.

At work today, _____

_____

_____

_____

_____

_____

_____

_____

_____I'm dumbemployed.

At work today, _____

_____

_____

_____

_____

_____

_____

_____

_____I'm dumbemployed.

At work today, _____

_____

_____

_____

_____

_____

_____

_____I'm dumbemployed.

ACKNOWLEDGMENTS

Phil Edwards would like to thank his mom and dad, who have supported him through hundreds of careers and an equal number of crises.

Matt Kraft would like to thank his mother and father, who always encouraged his attempts to avoid dumbemployment.

Both authors would like to thank Roseanne Wells for her dedication to this book and her unflagging tolerance of their awkwardness. Thanks also goes to Jordana Tusman for picking up and supporting this project, and to Bill Jones for taking on a big project and making it read effortlessly. And this book could not be possible without the counsel of Adam McNerney, who is a gentleman and scholar, a monk and a scoundrel, a saint and a sinner, and, most of all, a friend.

At work today, _____

_____

_____

_____

_____

_____

_____

_____

_____I'm dumbemployed.

At work today, _____

_____

_____

_____

_____

_____

_____

_____I'm dumbemployed.